I0224945

Karl Marx and Contemporary China

Chen Xueming

8th House Publishing

Canada

Cataloging in Publication (CIP) Data

Karl Marx and Contemporary China / By Chen Xueming

Chinese Version: China Renmin University Press, 2018.05

English Version: 8th House Publishing 2019.12

ISBN 978-1-7751040-5-6

Karl Marx and Contemporary China By Chen Xueming

Publication: 8th House Publishing

Region: Montreal, QC, Canada

Website: http://www.8thhousepublishing.com

Edition: 1st issue, May 2018 (Chinese)
      1st issue, December 2019 (English)

Impression: 1st print, December 2019

Copyright reserved.

China has stood up and got rich under the guidance of Marxism. While constructing this modernized strong country of socialism, which bears the mission of achieving the great rejuvenation of Chinese nation, Marxism has always been our powerful weapon of thoughts. And a strong China is inseparable from Marxist guidance. However, we cannot become indoctrinated Marxists; instead, China will make contribution to the development of Marxism, and push forward this theory into a new era.

Chen Xueming is a distinguished professor and doctoral supervisor at the School of Philosophy and School of Marxism, Fudan University. He is the Deputy Director of the Key Research Base of Humanities and Social Sciences of the Ministry of Education, Chief Expert of Shanghai Key Research Base of Humanities and Social Sciences, President of the National Contemporary Foreign Marxism Research Association, Vice President of the Marx and Engels Research Association of China, and Vice President of the China Society of Hominology. Professor Chen Xueming has led the completion of more than ten key research projects at or above the provincial and ministerial level, two of which are major projects of the National Social Science Foundation. He has published more than 30 books and textbooks, as well as more than 400 papers. In addition, Professor Chen Xueming has received nearly 20 awards at or above the provincial and ministerial level, including five first prizes for Shanghai Philosophy and Social Sciences Outstanding Achievements and Textbooks, one first prize (the seventh) and two second prizes (the fifth and fourth) of University Scientific Research Outstanding Achievement Award (Humanities and Social Sciences), one Five "One" Project Award and one China Excellent Publication Book Award (the sixth).

A Dialogue Crossing Time and Space

Historical events do not advance in straight lines; neither are they distributed evenly. The occurrence and fading of an event, and the birth and decease of a person, could both add to or decrease the weight of history. In the long historical river, some shiny eras and names always have great influence and are worth our memory. We honor historical persons and events at certain times to demonstrate our aspirations, hopes and historical understanding. We are actually adding to the weight of certain time periods in historical river. We explore and predict the future through dialogues crossing time and space.

Undoubtedly, the year 1818 became special because of Karl Marx's birth. Not long after, people have felt the weight of this historical giant on history, just as they felt the vacancy after his decease 65 years later. Almost every year, Marxist researchers could find important events commemorable in Marx's life. Those time-tested works have created different academical hot spots every year. However, this year is especially important, because it is the 200th anniversary of Marx's birth and the 170th anniversary of the issuance of *The Communist Manifesto*, which signifies the birth of Marxism; though the adoration of numbers is considered blind faith. And this year is the 40th anniversary of China's opening and reform as well as the issuance of *Practice Is The Sole Criterion for Testing Truth*, which marks the recovery of "being practical and realistic" in Marxism. These are all important and commemorable events. Commemoration is intended neither for forgetfulness nor for sheer memory. Commemoration and memory exist not only to write the conceptual history, but to expand key steps of history in a practical way. How we comprehend history will determine how we comprehend today and the future to arrive. By memorizing, awakening and reconstructing historical persons and events, we are walking hand-in-hand with those great persons, events and thoughts, which shall become the power we depend to walk into the future.

Now we are celebrating the 200th anniversary of Marx's birth and the 40th anniversary of China's opening and reform. These apparently independent commemoration activities are inherently and historically related. Since Marxism was spread into China and the Chinese Communist Party armed with Marxism became Chinese people's backbone, Marxism has been profoundly connected with the great rejuvenation of Chinese nation. Whenever we use the thought weapon of Marxism properly, we thrive in our national mission; and whenever we deviate from the principle of Marxism, we suffer setbacks, lose direction or even walk the path of wickedness. By adhering to Marxism and its Sinicization, Chinese Communists led Chinese people to stand up and make great achievements. Forty years ago, the "set things right" activity and opening and reform of China restored the guiding principle of "being practical and realistic", which is part of Marxism, and launched the 2nd historical phase of Marxism's Sinicization. Consequently, the Chinese Communists led people to get rich. Today, China is standing at a new historical starting point and welcoming new challenges of the times. Faced with new historical opportunities, China has started a new journey of hard work. At this moment, our commemoration of Karl Marx, *The Communist Manifesto*, the opening and reform, and *Practice Is The Sole Criterion for Testing Truth* has great significance. So far as we do it in a sincere and humble way, history will have nice arrangement for us, and we will gain wisdom by having dialogues with history, and be spiritually nourished for the journey in front of us.

A fundamental subject is carried through these commemoration activities. That is how to comprehend the relation between Marxism and modern China. Different perception of this issue will influence our commemoration in the aspect of standard, mood, purpose and the influence of commemoration itself, and will determine how we set foot on a new historical journey. Historical facts have proved that Marxism has played a fundamental role in Chinese people's journey of "standing up" and "getting rich". For today's China, the key to understanding Marxism and modern China is what kind of role Marxism plays in China's journey of getting strong. Is Marxism still necessary to guide China in this journey? How to adhere to Marxism as the guiding principle? In what aspects does Marxism guide this developing country? Only in-depth thinking and explanation of these questions can add weight to our commemoration activities, which will become historical events forming cohesive force, willpower and mobilization.

Needless to say, there are a lot of inaccurate and erroneous understandings on the relation between Marxism and modern China. Generally, they include the sayings of contradiction, foreign introduction, outdatedness and lack of necessity. If we honor Marx and the opening and reform of China with the above sayings, we are actually departing from Marxism, and our commemoration will be intended for departure and the drawing of a clear boundary line between Marxism and modern China. We surely stand in opposition to these mistaken sayings, but this book is not intended to criticize them, either. Neither our practice nor the basis of methodology has provided value for such criticism. The above mistaken sayings only reflect biases of standing or metaphysical and non-dialectical thinking on the relation between theory, practice, history and reality. Objectively, Marxism has formed the structure of modern China, and we have become heirs to the heritage of Marxism, if viewing from the angle of world history. And we are living in the history of Marxism. China's success of "standing up" and "getting rich" has proved and will continue to prove that Marxism is a strong weapon of thought for Chinese nation to rejuvenate itself. To adhere to

Marxism as the guiding principle is the fundamental guarantee for constructing a socialist modern country.

However, we cannot become indoctrinated Marxists. Marxism is guiding China's practice, and meanwhile, China's practice is contributing to Marxism's development. Pushing forward Sinicization and modernization of Marxism is the basic strategy of defeating dogmatism and nihilism, and will form a historical logic to help us adhere to and develop Marxism. Theory, practice, history and reality always expand in the form of dialectical dialogue. Marxism can only lead the times and become their banners in the process of opening and progressing. We will commemorate Marx and the country's opening and reform in the form of a dialogue crossing time and space, and explain how Marxism is guiding China still even if it has become strong.

End of preface.

TABLE OF CONTENTS

PRESIDENT XI JINPING. SOCIALISM WITH CHINESE CHARACTERISTICS CENTERED ON PRESIDENT XI JINPING IS THE LATEST THEORETICAL RESULT OF SINICIZATION OF MARXISM.

(II) THE CHINESE NATION REJUVENATED ITSELF BY "GETTING RICH AND STRONG", AS A CONSEQUENCE OF GLOBAL JUDGMENT OF CHINA'S SOCIAL AND HISTORICAL ORIENTATION FROM THE PERSPECTIVE OF HISTORICAL MATERIALISM.

(III) IN THE NEW ERA OF "GETTING STRONG", WE SHOULD ADHERE TO MARXIST PRINCIPLE ON MANY SIDES, ENSURE THE SUCCESS OF SOCIALIST CONSTRUCTION, AND IMPROVE MARXISM IN THE NEW HISTORICAL STAGE.

(I) REALITY HAS PROVED THAT CCP'S LEADERSHIP IS CRUCIAL FOR SOCIALISM WITH CHINESE CHARACTERISTICS IN THE NEW ERA.

(II) ACCORDING TO WORDS OF MARXISM ON PROLETARIAT POLITICAL PARTIES, THE PURPOSE OF CCP HAS DETERMINED ITS LEGITIMACY OF LEADERSHIP.

(III) ACCORDING TO MARXIST THEORIES ON THE MASSES, CLASSES, POLITICAL PARTIES AND LEADERS, THE AUTHORITY OF THE PARTY CENTRAL

COMMITTEE CENTERED ON MR. XI JINPING MUST BE MAINTAINED TO BUILD A STRONG CHINA.

(IV) THE PARTY CENTRAL COMMITTEE CENTERED ON MR. XI JINPING GOVERNS THE PARTY STRICTLY ACCORDING TO THE PARTY CONSTRUCTION THEORY OF MARXISM, AND GUARANTEES THAT THE PARTY CAN LEAD CHINESE PEOPLE TO "GET STRONG".

IV. "GETTING STRONG" REQUIRES TREMENDOUS POWER: INSEPARABLE FROM THE PEOPLE'S PRINCIPAL POSITION THEORY OF MARXISM86

(I) IN ESSENCE, THE MATERIALIST CONCEPTION OF HISTORY IS A PEOPLE'S CONCEPTION. WE MUST ADHERE TO THE PEOPLE'S PRINCIPAL POSITION THEORY OF MARXISM, WHICH IS BASED ON THE PEOPLE'S CONCEPTION OF HISTORY IN ORDER TO ACHIEVE THE GREAT REJUVENATION OF CHINESE NATION

(II) TO ACHIEVE THE GREAT REJUVENATION OF CHINESE NATION, WE MUST DEFEND THE PEOPLE'S DEMOCRATIC RIGHTS, PROMOTE SOCIALIST DEMOCRACY, AND TRANSFORM OUR COUNTRY INTO A SOCIALIST, DEMOCRATIC AND MODERNIZED STRONG COUNTRY.

(III) TO ACHIEVE THE GREAT MISSION OF "GETTING STRONG", WE SHOULD PROTECT PEOPLE'S DEMOCRATIC RIGHTS, REGARD THE FUNDAMENTAL INTERESTS OF THE PEOPLE AS THE HIGHEST

STANDARD, AND WIN THE PEOPLE'S LOVE AND SUPPORT.

(IV) TO "GET STRONG", WE MUST MOTIVATE PEOPLE TO ENGAGE IN CONSTRUCTION AS A PRINCIPAL PART. CONSCIOUS PARTICIPATION OF THE PEOPLE IS A PRINCIPAL GUARANTEE FOR CONSTRUCTING A SOCIALIST AND MODERNIZED STRONG COUNTRY.

V. "GETTING STRONG" REQUIRES A SPIRITUAL PILLAR: INSEPARABLE FROM THE GUIDANCE OF MARXIST IDEOLOGICAL THEORIES 118

(I) ACCORDING TO MARXIST IDEOLOGICAL THEORY, THERE IS THE DIALECTICAL MOVEMENT OF "ECONOMIC BASE - SUPERSTRUCTURE" IN HUMAN SOCIETY. IDEOLOGY REFLECTS AND PUSHES FORWARD SOCIAL DEVELOPMENT, AND ESPECIALLY, MARXISM HAS SUCH REALISTIC POWER.

(II) ACCORDING TO MARXIST IDEOLOGICAL THEORY, IDEOLOGY ULTIMATELY REFLECTS ECONOMIC BASE, AND WE SHOULD COPE WITH THE SIGNIFICANT TRANSFORMATION OF CHINESE ECONOMIC SOCIETY IN A PROPER WAY. BY STAYING TRUE TO OUR MISSION AND KEEPING PACE WITH THE TIMES, WE SHOULD ASSERT MARXISM'S GUIDING POSITION IN THE IDEOLOGICAL FIELD.

(III) MARXIST IDEOLOGICAL THEORY CAN BE USED TO REVEAL THE FALSEHOOD OF

"WESTERNIZATION" AND THE SO-CALLED "UNIVERSAL VALUE", AND DEMONSTRATE THE CHINESE WISDOM SUITABLE FOR THE NATIONAL CONDITIONS AND SOCIAL SYSTEM OF CHINA.

(IV) ACCORDING TO MARXIST IDEOLOGICAL THEORY, WE SHOULD GUARD AGAINST CULTURAL CONSERVATISM, AND SHOULD CRITICIZE, INHERIT AND DEVELOP TRADITIONAL CHINESE CULTURE AS PART OF THE SOCIALIST CULTURE WITH CHINESE CHARACTERISTICS.

(V) SEVERAL IMPORTANT PRINCIPLES REQUIRED TO ADHERE TO THE GUIDING POSITION OF MARXISM IN IDEOLOGICAL FIELD.

VI. TO "GET STRONG", CHINA NEEDS TO FACE MODERNITY PROPERLY: INSEPARABLE FROM THE GUIDANCE OF MARXIST MODERNITY CRITICISM THEORY 150

(I) ACCORDING TO MARXIST MODERNITY CRITICISM THEORY, MODERNITY IS A WHOLE, AND CHINA CANNOT STAY IN "PARTIAL MODERNITY". WE CAN ONLY "GET STRONG" BY ACHIEVING MODERNITY COMPREHENSIVELY.

(II) ACCORDING TO MARXIST MODERNITY CRITICISM THEORY, STRONG NEGATIVE EFFECTS WILL BE PRODUCED DURING THE ROLL-OUT OF MODERNITY, AND CHINA MUST CONFRONT THESE NEGATIVE EFFECTS AND OVERCOME THEM IN ORDER TO "GET STRONG".

(III) ACCORDING TO MARXIST MODERNITY CRITICISM THEORY, MODERNITY CAN BE SURPASSED, AND CHINA MUST SURPASS MODERNITY WHILE ACHIEVING IT. BY SURPASSING MODERNITY, IT WILL REALLY "GET STRONG".

(IV) ACCORDING TO MARXIST MODERNITY CRITICISM THEORY, MODERNITY MUST BE INVOLVED IN VARIOUS COMPLEX RELATIONSHIPS. SO CHINA MUST DOMINATE VARIOUS CONTRADICTIONS PROPERLY BASED ON COMPLEX MODERNITY IN ORDER TO "GET STRONG".

VII. GREAT POWER DIPLOMACY IS REQUIRED TO "GET STRONG": INSEPARABLE FROM THE GUIDANCE OF MARXIST WORLD HISTORY THEORY   184

(I) MARXISM IS A TOTALITY THEORY BASED ON TOTALIZATION OF HUMAN SOCIETY. A STRONG CHINA NEEDS GREAT POWER DIPLOMACY, SO IT MUST CONTINUE TO OPEN UP BY FOLLOWING THE GUIDANCE OF MARXIST WORLD HISTORY THEORY.

(II) A STRONG CHINA SHALL ADHERE TO THE DIPLOMATIC PRINCIPLE OF INDEPENDENCE, AND SHALL NOT IMPOSE ON OTHER COUNTRIES ITS UNIQUE EXPERIENCE OR MODEL WITH NATIONAL POWER.

(III) A STRONG CHINA SHALL CONTRIBUTE TO THE CONSTRUCTION OF NEW INTERNATIONAL RELATIONSHIPS OF MUTUAL RESPECT, FAIRNESS, JUSTICE AND WIN-WIN COOPERATION BY FOLLOWING THE PATHWAY OF PEACEFUL

DEVELOPMENT UNDER THE GUIDANCE OF MARXIST WAR AND PEACE PRINCIPLE.

(IV) ACHIEVING FREE AND COMPREHENSIVE DEVELOPMENT OF HUMANS BY USING MARXISM AND CONSTRUCTING A COMMUNITY OF SHARED FUTURE FOR MANKIND IS AN IMPORTANT PROPOSITION OF 21ST CENTURY IN CHINESE MARXISM.

(I) MARXISM HAS SCIENTIFICALLY REMOLDED THE COMMUNIST THEORY BY TARGETING THE PROBLEMS AND SICKNESS OF CAPITALIST SOCIETY. BASED ON THE CURRENT STAGE OF DEVELOPMENT, CHINA UNIFIED THE HIGHEST PRINCIPLE OF COMMUNISM AND THE CURRENT HISTORICAL TASK. THE COUNTRY WALKS THE PATH OF SOCIALISM WITH CHINESE CHARACTERISTICS AND SURPASSES OTHER COUNTRIES IN THE ASPECT OF MODERNIZATION.

(II) IN THE PROCESS OF "GETTING STRONG", CHINA IS DEDICATED TO REALIZING THE DREAM OF COMMUNISM AND PUSHING FORWARD "THE GREAT STRUGGLE" AND "GREAT SOCIALIST REVOLUTION".

(III) FACED WITH MISUNDERSTANDINGS, DISTORTIONS AND ATTACKS, CHINA SHOULD RAISE THE FLAG OF SCIENTIFIC SOCIALISM IN THE 21ST CENTURY, PROVE THE PRACTICABILITY OF

COMMUNISM BY USING MARXIST THEORY, AND WHILE "GETTING STRONG", IT SHOULD CONTRIBUTE ITS SOLUTIONS TO THE WORLD.

(IV) THE GREATEST CONTRIBUTION OF SOCIALISM WITH CHINESE CHARACTERISTICS TO COMMUNISM IS ITS PRACTICE, WHICH HAS VIVIDLY DEMONSTRATED HOW A SOCIALIST COUNTRY OPERATES.

IX. CORRECT METHODOLOGY IS REQUIRED TO "GET STRONG": INSEPARABLE FROM THE GUIDANCE OF MARXIST METHODOLOGY 249

(I) MARXISM IS A WORLDVIEW SURPASSING IDEALISM AND OLD MATERIALISM. TO FOLLOW MARXIST IDEOLOGY, WE MUST ADHERE TO THE BASIC WORLDVIEW OF MARXISM.

(II) TO "GET STRONG", WE SHOULD ADHERE TO THE IDEOLOGICAL PRINCIPLE OF "BEING PRACTICAL AND REALISTIC" IN MARXISM, COMBINE THEORY AND PRACTICE, AND AVOID SUBJECTIVISM AND DOGMATISM.

(III) TO "GET STRONG", CHINA SHOULD ALWAYS USE MARXIST HISTORICAL ANALYSIS, VIEW EVENTS AND SOCIAL AND HISTORICAL DEVELOPMENT WITH HISTORICAL AND DEVELOPMENTAL INSIGHT, AND OBJECT TO COMPLACENT, CONSERVATIVE, AND RIGID ATTITUDES.

(IV) IN THE PROCESS OF "GETTING STRONG", CHINA SHOULD ALWAYS USE TOTALITY THINKING OF MARXISM IN ORDER TO ACCURATELY

UNDERSTAND THE HISTORICAL ORIENTATION AND SIGNIFICANCE OF SOCIALISM WITH CHINESE CHARACTERISTICS IN THE NEW ERA.

(I) A COMMUNITY OF SHARED FUTURE FOR MANKIND WAS FIRST PROPOSED IN SOCIALISM WITH CHINESE CHARACTERISTICS IN THE NEW AGE CENTERED ON PRESIDENT XI JINPING. IT IS AN IMPORTANT PROPOSITION OF MARXISM IN THE 21ST CENTURY, AND HAS PROVIDED NEW CONNOTATIONS FOR THE PURPOSE "FREE AND COMPREHENSIVE DEVELOPMENT OF HUMANS".

(II) PUSH FORWARD HUMAN DEVELOPMENT BY REJUVENATING THE CHINESE NATION. THE CONCEPT OF HUMAN LIBERATION IN MARXISM HAS BEEN IMPLEMENTED IN A NATIONAL STATE.

(III) THE SOCIAL CONSTRUCTION THEORY OF MARXISM IN PEACEFUL TIMES IS ENRICHED THROUGH THE ACT OF CONSTRUCTING A COMMUNITY OF SHARED FUTURE FOR MANKIND, STRENGTHENING A COMMUNITY OF CHINESE NATION, AND PUSHING MARXISM INTO A NEW HISTORICAL PERIOD OF PEACEFUL DEVELOPMENT.

(IV) THE STRONG CHINA HAS INSPIRED MARXISTS TO SUBJECTIVELY CREATE HISTORY, TRANSFORM THEIR REVOLUTION SPIRIT INTO STRONG POWER IN THE PRACTICE OF PEACEFUL CONSTRUCTION, AND

MAKE CONTRIBUTION TO THE ADVANCEMENT OF HUMAN SOCIETY.

I

Chinese civilization is one of the four greatest ancient civilizations and has lasted over 5,000 years. At the most times of human history, China has been leading the world in politics, economy, science and technology, and has contributed enormously to human civilization. However, this great empire has seemed to decline since the First Opium War opened its doors. During the period of change which never happened before, China gradually became a semi-colonial and semi-feudal society, and Chinese people was forced into a tragic situation on the verge of distinction. Why did such a brilliant country become so fragile and fall in danger? After exploring many different paths, China finally "stood up", "got rich" and "became strong". What kind of miraculous power rescued China? And what kind of theory guided Chinese people out of decline and onto the journey of rejuvenation? The Party's 19th National Congress has clearly pointed out: "China's revolutionary pioneers saw a solution in Marxism-Leninism." During tireless exploration, Chinese

Communist Party armed with Marxist theory was founded, and since then, "Chinese people had a backbone in its struggle for national independence, liberation, wealth and happiness, and their position turned from passive to active." Since its foundation, CCP became the backbone of the great rejuvenation of Chinese nation. It led Chinese people from passive position to active position, and from revolution and construction to reforms. Step by step, it realized the dream of national rejuvenation. History has clearly proved that the guiding position of Marxism is the fundamental guarantee for our success in revolution, construction and reforms. In new historical conditions, properly understanding the relationship between Marxism and modern China, and adhering to the guiding position of Marxism in construction of socialism with Chinese characteristics is the basic need of our country to "get strong" in the new times and rejuvenate itself. "Marxism and its development in China has provided the most advanced and appropriate scientific theory for the development of the Party and people's cause, and provided a solid foundation of thought for the unity of the Party and people of all ethnics. Marxism is the basic guideline for the Party and our country. If we deviate from or abandon Marxism, our Party will lose its soul and direction. As far as Marxist guidance is concerned, we must always stand firm without any shaking." We use Marxism to review the past and look at the future. Adhering to the guiding position of Marxism while avoiding dogmatism, and innovating and developing Marxism in practice is the basic requirement for Chinese Communists to lead Chinese people in its pathway of national rejuvenation.

It was said Napoleon once called China a sleeping eastern lion, and warned Britain not to startle this lion, because once it woke up, it would shake the entire world. This analogy turned into an accurate prediction. In the next 100 years, this eastern lion was bullied, woke up and shook the world. What kind of spiritual strength awakened and armed this big lion so that it would return to the center of world stage with tremendous power upon its awakening? Hegel, who was contemporary with Napoleon, also had a similar statement. As he said in *Philosophy of History*, ancient Chinese history represents the childhood of human development during which objective existence and subjective movement was not contradicted, therefore it is a stagnant history without real change, or called "history of non-history". According to Hegel's view, Chinese history lacks subjectivity, and it would truly merges into world history only with the participation of many positive elements. To some extent, Hegel's historical view was influenced by Eurocentrism, but his belief that China's historical development requires activation by a subjective spirit of the times was indeed profound. Once the spiritual sunshine was cast upon this sleeping land, it will revitalize everything into booming development, and opens up an entirely new world. And the modern history of China is how this country was bullied by powers, how the people fought against monarchy and feudal customs and awakened in national and democratic spirit, and how this country walked from sleep and decline into independence, strength and rejuvenation.

Before the Opium War, China was a feudal empire highly centralized in power. There was a huge surplus in foreign trade, and China's economic aggregate was top of the world. However, through the intense capitalist revolution and the first industrial revolution, western capitalist countries developed rapidly and opened a new page of human history. Meanwhile, the Qing empire was in slumber in the sweet dream of Great Empire. It closed the country, regarded itself as the best, and fell behind gradually. The decline was not only in the aspect of economy or military, but in the times, because China's social form and spiritual principles were lagging behind history. Because of overall decline, the huge empire was, surprisingly, defeated over and over again. After territory ceding, payment of indemnities, opening of ports and businesses, a series of unequal treaties were forced upon Chinese people, and China gradually fell into a semi-colonial and semi-feudal society. Under power invasion and the impact of modern capitalist civilization, Chinese people started difficult exploration. Before the start of new democratic revolution, various social strengths put forward different plans of saving the country, but all of them failed. "After the Opium War, China was plunged into a dark period of internal struggles and external disturbances, and Chinese people experienced the misery of wars, splits and poverty. To rejuvenate the nation, countless heroic and compassionate people fought continuously with their ambition. They tried different ways, but still could not change the social quality of old China and Chinese people's miserable fate."

Faced with internal struggles and external disturbances caused by failure in Opium War, the peasant class rose up and fought against injustice, represented by the Taiping Rebellion led by Hong Xiuquan and Boxing Rebellion afterwards. Due to restrictions of peasant thinking, they did not solve China's poverty and weakness according to modern principles; and their rebellions were conservative at the root. Hong Xiuquan, leader of Taiping Rebellion only imagined to overthrow the dynasty and open a new one like many emperors did in the past, and could not fulfill the mission of overthrowing monarchy and feudal customs; not to mention the Boxing Rebellion, which had neither guidelines nor organization. Different from the peasant class, the open-minded feudal official class also launched a westernization movement aimed at self-rescue and self-strengthening from the 1860s to the Sino-Japanese War. They still hold the dream of Great Empire, and with the slogans of "self-strengthening" and "getting rich", they developed national capital and military companies under the guidance of "borrowing the west to enrich China" and almost on the basis of "learning from foreigners to compete with them". They considered the advancement of capitalism as a "technique" on the level of tools, and tried to rescue the Qing court by introducing western military equipment, machine production, science and technology. But they only saw the aspect of western advancement in tools and tried to strengthen and rescue the court without changing its system; as a result, their failure was shown in Sino-Japanese Naval War. In such circumstances, constitutional reform was put on the schedule, and the reformists went onto the historical stage of saving the country. The reformists realized the advancement of modern capitalist civilization and tried to set up a constitutional monarchy with the royal support, change the national system which was unfit for modern development, and implement reforms in politics, economy and culture, but their efforts failed completely under the besiege of conservative strength. Two years later, the invasion of Eight-Power Allied Forces and war indemnities forced China into a semi-colonial and semi-feudal society on the verge of extinction. Under such extreme conditions,

Qing rulers' preparatory constitutionalism was too weak to maintain, and the feudal system of 2,000 years was finally overthrown by the revolutionaries.

During the explorations and failures, the capitalist revolutionaries represented by Sun Zhongshan walked to the historical front line. The revolutionaries founded a revolutionary party with clear guidelines, and hoped to overthrow feudal autocracy through revolution and found a capitalist republic with a presidential system. After several failed battles, the Wuchang Uprising made a success in 1911, and the leader Sun Zhongshan assumed the presidential office in Nanjing in 1912. Thus, a capitalist republic was founded. Although the 1911 Revolution overthrew the Chinese feudal system having lasted 2,000 years, the fruit of revolution was stolen by Yuan Shikai. Yuan Shikai went against the historical current in a failed attempt to restore monarchy as the emperor, and the nation was again put into war and chaos. The system of capitalist democratic republic proved a failure in China. Neither feudal powers and their remaining forces nor the colonists wished to see China getting strong through a democratic republic system. While apparently supporting the revolution, they were using and supporting the conservative forces and acting against revolution to assure their interests. Therefore, a capitalist revolution targeting the feudal autocracy but not the imperialists could not make a success. As Mr. Mao Zedong pointed out, the invasion of imperialism, the adherent nature of comprador capitalist class and the weakness of national capitalist class had deprived China of the global and domestic conditions for setting up and developing a capitalist system.

However, China's history of disasters was the same history of rescue by various forces, and of people's awakening. Throughout peasant revolution, the westernization movement led by feudal officials, the constitutional reform of capitalist reformists and the revolution of revolutionaries, various forces went onto stage and various ideas were put forward; though brilliant, they could not lead Chinese people onto the path of national rejuvenation. The root cause was in their historical limitations. These forces and ideas were separate from Chinese social nature, the major task of reforms and revolution, and scientific theoretical guideline, therefore they could not invite massive people's participation. In this regard, Mao Zedong had an in-depth analysis: "During the 70 years from the Opium War in 1840 to the May 4th Movement in 1919, Chinese people had no thought weapon to resist imperialism. The stubborn feudalism collapsed after failed wars. With no other resorts, Chinese people learned from imperialism in the old days -- western capitalist revolution -- theory of evolution, theory of natural rights, and capitalist republic's thought weapon and political solutions. They organized political parties, conducted revolutions, and believed they would defend against powers and establish a stable republic. But all that stuff was as weak as feudalism and collapsed at the end."

Due to lack of advanced leadership armed with pioneering thinking, these struggles, though brilliant, could not change the miserable fate of our nation. Only by reviewing the difficult struggles in history can we really comprehend the guiding position of Marxism and CCP as people's choice. Since the October Revolution brought about Marxism-Leninism, China's revolution opened a new page. Marxism was introduced into

China and awakened the subjective spirit of Chinese people to rise up and create history. It really awakened this big lion and created new circumstances for national development.

While Chinese people were strenuously exploring ways of rescuing the country, the First World War broke out due to unbalanced development and interest disputes among major capitalist countries. War caused revolutions in the weakest part of imperialism. The triumph of October Socialist Revolution opened a new page in human history. Since then, proletarian revolution went onto historical stage, and the anti-feudal capitalist revolution was no longer the historical direction. In other words, through Marxist criticism against modern capitalism, the historical limitation of capitalism was clearly revealed. Therefore, the fight against feudalism and founding of a capitalist democratic republic in the new historical period only replaced the old rule with more equal and democratic governance, and had made no real advancement. But the October Revolution surpassed modern capitalism and set out a new direction toward socialism and communism. It heralded the coming of a new social period. More importantly, October Revolution made a success in Russia, a country as poor and backward as China to set an example for Chinese people's revolution. Russia's October Revolution shone new light on China, which was exploring its way in darkness.

Mao Zedong said: "The October Revolution in 1917 awakened Chinese people to Marxism-Leninism, which was new on that date." During the period, Russia was still a developing country in capitalist economy, and its social and economic development was on the same level as China. Although Russia did not fall, like China, into a semi-colonial and semi-feudal society, it was still in a semi-feudal state. The October Revolution's success in backward Russia set an example for Chinese people, and through propagation activities carried out by intellectuals, Chinese people's revolutionary enthusiasm was lit up. Besides, October Revolution was against capitalism, so it enabled open-minded Chinese intellectuals to realize that the invasion of developed capitalist countries was the root cause for all disasters, and founding a capitalist democratic republic could not brought China with real advancement. And the imperialist powers tried hard to impede the progress of capitalist revolution for their own gain. China must act against imperialism, or capitalist powers in order to gain victory. In this scenario, Chinese intellectuals concluded that we must "learn from Russia", and believed China should walk the socialist path, too. In terms of the transition from capitalist trend to socialism, Qu Qiubai analyzed: "Chinese nation has been exploited over the past decades, and now it is tasting the bitterness of a colony. The suppression of imperialism ended the nightmare of vacant nationalism, and also led to student movements and the Shandong issue. Industrially developed countries' modern problem is capitalism, or imperialism in their colonies, therefore the student movements turned their direction to socialism."

The victory of October Revolution not only awakened Chinese people, but brought us Marxism-Leninism, and a whole new theory, thought system and direction for Chinese revolution. Since then, Chinese revolution turned from old democratism to new democracy. In this regard, the 19th National Congress of the Party made a brilliant statement: "A hundred years ago, the October Revolution brought China with the gift of

Marxism-Leninism. Open-minded Chinese intellectuals saw a solution to China's problems in the truth of Marxism-Leninism. During the drastic movements of Chinese society in modern periods, Chinese people's fierce fight against feudal rule and foreign invasions, and the combination of Marxism-Leninism with Chinese worker movements, the Chinese Communist Party was founded in 1912. Since then, Chinese people had a backbone in their struggle for national independence, people's liberation, nation's prosperity and people's happiness. And Chinese people turned from a passive position to active." Certainly, October Revolution only brought about a general theory. To make the theory work and solve actual problems in China, it must be integrated into Chinese reality and sinicized. Chinese revolution had its own specific scenario, objectives and tasks. Applying the general principles of Marxism and the pathway of October Revolution mechanically and in defiance of China's actual situation had caused setbacks in Chinese revolution.

The new democratic revolution is a basic theory of Chinese revolution creatively put forward by Mao

Zedong when he combined Marxist revolution theory with China's reality, and is the basic result of the first leap of Marxism's Sinicization and the core content of Mao Zedong thought. The new democratic revolution is the people's democratic revolution led by the proletarian class against imperialism, feudalism and bureaucrat capitalism. China's new democratic revolution was different from the capitalist democratic revolution targeting only the feudal system and the proletarian revolution targeting only the capitalists. Besides fighting against imperialism and feudalism, China was also on the mission of overthrowing bureaucrat capitalism. Both the fight against imperialism and bureaucrat capitalism had the objective of opposing and surpassing capitalism. Therefore, new democratic revolution was a national democratic revolution aiming to realize socialism and communism, but its precondition was to accomplish people's liberation from feudalism and national independence from imperialism. This was determined by the nature of a semi-colonial and semi-feudal society, and the bureaucrat capitalism in which the bureaucrat class colluded with capital. Consequently, the initiatives of the peasant class, feudal official class, capitalist class and bureaucrat capitalist class could never fit into China's situation. In the complex Chinese society, they use only one force against another, and some of them were sources of disaster themselves, therefore they could not thoroughly solve China's problems and lead Chinese people to fulfill the great mission of self-rescue and national rejuvenation. Only the new democratic revolution with the participation of the masses led by worker class could set out the goals to fight against imperialism, feudalism and bureaucrat capitalism and achieve victory of revolution. "Our Party has profoundly realized that Chinese people must remove the three burdens -- imperialism, feudalism and bureaucrat capitalism -- in order to achieve national rejuvenation, national independence, people's liberation, national unity and social stability. Under our leadership, the people found the correct path of revolution by encircling the city from villages and stepping into power by armed forces. After 28 years of painstaking wars, we completed the new democratic revolution, founded the People's Public of China in 1949, and accomplished the great leap from feudal autocracy to people's democracy."

Combining Marxist theory with China's revolutionary practice, putting forward our own revolutionary theory and walking our own revolutionary path had been the fundamental guarantee for our victory in revolution. As Mr. Mao Zedong pointed out: "October Revolution helped the entire world and China's open-minded individuals to observe a country's fate with the proletarian cosmology and reconsider their own problems. Walking the path of Russians -- this is the conclusion." The path of Russians is the theoretical path of Marxism, or the socialist path. This is the conclusion. Meanwhile, we should build our own path by observing our own issues with proletarian cosmology. It is the problem of dialectical relation between adherence and development. The guidance of Marxism for Chinese revolution was realized through Marxism's Sinicization. Only sinicized Marxism can be used to guide China's practice, and we should not only copy the Marxist doctrine. Just as Marx himself said: "Theory works in a specific country only to the extent it meets the needs of this country." We can only apply and realize a theory based on our country's actual needs. We learn from Russia and adhere to Marxist guideline only on the levels of worldview and methodology; and should not copy the theory and Russian model mechanically. On the early days of revolution, we had setbacks because of indiscriminate copying. The Chinese Communists represented by Mao Zedong adhered to the theoretical guidance of Marxism, summed up experience in practice, accomplished Marxism's Sinicization and opened up the brilliant path of "encircling the city from villages and stepping into power by armed forces." Adhering to Marxism in both theory and practice and accomplishing Marxism's Sinicization was Mao Zedong's important contribution to Marxism's Sinicization and the entire Marxism. As Mao Zedong pointed out: "Marxism without Chinese characteristics is but vacant and abstract. Therefore, how to implement Marxism in China according to Chinese characteristics is an imperative issue of our Party."

Mr. Deng Xiaoping pointed out: "If we were not Marxists and did not have sufficient faith in Marxism, or did not combine Marxism with China's reality, or did not walk our own path, China's revolution could not make a success, and China would still be split, dependent and disunited. Faith in Marxism is a spiritual force for Chinese people to achieve victory in revolution." Mao Zedong thought is the first theoretical form of sinicized Marxism created in revolutionary war. Under the guidance of Mao Zedong thought, CCP led Chinese people to gain victory in new democratic revolution, found a new China, "stand up", rejuvenate the Chinese nation, and achieve national independence and people's democracy. Any viewpoint denying Marxism's guiding position in Chinese revolution or Mao Zedong's historical merits was actually a form of nihilism. When Mr. Xi Jinping was celebrating the 95th anniversary of CCP's foundation, he highly praised our Party's historical contribution: "This great contribution is that our Party led Chinese people through 28 years of painstaking war to defeat Japanese imperialism, overthrow the reactionary rule of Nationalist Party, complete new democratic revolution and found the People's Republic of China. CCP put an end to our semi-colonial and semi-feudal state, the scattered forces of old China, and the unequal treaties and imperial privileges imposed on China, and accomplished the great leap from feudal autocratic politics of several thousand years to people's democracy." The leap, in essence, helped Chinese nation to stand up after an arduous process of rejuvenation, and provided a historical precondition and basis for this country to "get rich and strong".

However, despite the great and brilliant history, a tendency of nihilism once appeared to darken and distort history in the name of objective research. They considered revolutionary struggle as inhumane violence, denied the guiding position of Marxism and CCP's merits in anti-Japanese War, criticized and cursed revolutionary heroes and leaders, and produced a very negative influence. To objectively evaluate the revolutionary history from the standpoint of historical materialism, realistically evaluate the great merits of revolution, and object to distortions, darkening and attacks is the basic guarantee for us to walk into the future. A nation without objective evaluation of their own history or respect for their own heroes is a nation without hope. If we darken our history and despise heroes, we will lose our future, so we must resolutely criticize such behavior. The Chinese nation must adhere to the guiding position of Marxism and the proper viewpoint of historical materialism on China's revolutionary history and theory of "standing up" in order to rejuvenate the Chinese civilization and "get strong".

After the founding of new China, our Party carried out arduous explorations and practice in socialist construction. It made great achievements and accumulated rich experience and profound lessons. Under the Party's leadership, we quickly recovered national economic production, accomplished socialist transformation, and set up various basic systems of socialism. But in the following practice, "Because the Party made a "left" deviation in thought, many proper guidelines of socialist construction were not implemented, and we even experienced a nationwide and long-term mistake -- "cultural revolution". All of these were severe setbacks in socialist construction." Since the opening and reform of the country, the 2nd generation of Party leaders centered on Deng Xiaoping followed the principle of "being practical and realistic", thoroughly denied the wrong path of "class struggle as the topmost priority", set things right, and objectively evaluated Mao Zedong's historical position. Thus, the Party opened a new page of national rejuvenation.

While discussing the truth, CCP recovered Mr. Mao Zedong's Marxist guideline of "being practical and realistic", concluded the theme of the times as transformation from war and revolution to peace and development, and determined that Chinese society was in the beginning stage of socialism. Based on the above judgments, we decisively abandoned class struggle and continuous revolution, placed economic construction at the center, adhered to the opening and reform of the country as well as the four basic principles as the basic guideline in the beginning stage of socialism. It was called Deng Xiaoping theory. Deng Xiaoping theory became our practical guideline for socialist construction in the new era. "Mr. Deng Xiaoping first systematically responded to basic questions including how to construct socialism in such a economically and culturally backward country as China, and how to strengthen and develop socialism. He inherited and developed Marxism with new views, uplifted Marxism to a new level, and enriched our understanding of socialism. By creating the Deng Xiaoping theory, he set out the pathway of socialism with Chinese characteristics." If we say Mao Zedong thought is sinicized Marxism centered on revolution and the first leap of Marxism's Sinicization; then Deng Xiaoping theory is sinicized Marxism centered on reforms and the second leap and second theoretical result of Marxism's Sinicization. Under the guidance of the above theory, China went through 40 years of reform and opening, and eventually became rich and strong. It marched one big step forward on the pathway of national rejuvenation.

While talking about the great journey of opening and reform, Mr. Xi Jinping pointed out: "In the beginning of opening and reform, our Party made a great call of walking our own path and constructing socialism with Chinese characteristics. Since then, our Party led all ethnics of our country to strive forward. We squeezed into the top list of the world in economy, technology, national defense and comprehensive strength. We made unprecedented progress in international position. The appearance of the Party, our country, the people, the military and Chinese nation changed dramatically. And we are standing in the east with an entirely new posture." In the new historical period, "Our Party deeply realized that we must follow the trend, obey people's will, bravely open up and reform, and continuously push forward our cause in order to rejuvenate the Chinese nation. Our Party leads people to open up and reform the country, remove all obstacles in thought and systems, build the pathway of socialism with Chinese characteristics, and keep pace with the times." The great practice of opening and reform was carried out under the guidance of sinicized Marxism. And the basic guideline for the beginning stage of socialism was to follow Marxism as the basic political principle.

This year is the 40th anniversary of the truth discussion and opening and reform, the 200th anniversary of Marx' birth and the 170th anniversary of the publication of *The Communist Manifesto*. Commemoration activities are being held across the country. Practically speaking, it is very important to know how to evaluate the historical significance of the 40 years' reform, and how to understand the relationship between Deng Xiaoping theory, Marxism, and Mao Zedong thought. Undoubtedly, there were some wrong inclinations in our understanding. Those inclined toward Mao Zedong thought often take lightly or belittle Deng Xiaoping's theoretical contribution, and neglect the difference between Deng Xiaoping theory and Mao Zedong thought. They always try to seek the root of Deng Xiaoping theory in Mao Zedong thought, and emphasize that Deng Xiaoping's correct understandings are already contained in Mao Zedong thought, and Deng Xiaoping had nothing new to offer. Some people are just to the contrary. They try to set out a boundary line between Deng Xiaoping theory and Mao Zedong thought. They only saw the difference and deny the internal relation between both in order to criticize Deng Xiaoping theory and the pathway of reform and opening, believing that such a path has deviated from Mao Zedong thought, Marxism and socialism. Different from those who abstractly affirm Mao Zedong thought, some others are inclined to affirm Deng Xiaoping theory. They also emphasize the difference between the two in order to highlight the great contribution and uniqueness of Deng Xiaoping theory. They use Deng Xiaoping theory to deny Mao Zedong thought, and use the opening and reform to deny the 30 years prior to that, and even deny the entire revolutionary history, believing that the opening and reform enables China to abandon the concept of revolution and return to the correct pathway of human civilization. They are actually affirming Deng Xiaoping theory and its value based on the denial of Mao Zedong thought and Marxism. In essence, it is not an affirmation, but destruction and distortion of Deng Xiaoping theory.

Our Party has always been looking at the development of Marxism and Chinese Marxism from a dialectical and historical perspective; therefore, we neither deny the past nor linger; instead, we keep pace with the times, follow the trend and become pioneers. While evaluating the relation between Deng Xiaoping theory and Mao Zedong thought, we adhere to the principle of "being practical and realistic" and the dialectical view of development. We neither use Mao Zedong thought to deny Deng Xiaoping theory nor the other way around. We don't deny the period after opening and reform with the merits prior to that; nor do we deny the period before opening and reform with the merits after that. We emphasize inheritance and development, and see both similarities and differences. If we only see the former, we would belittle or negate the great contribution of Mr. Deng Xiaoping. On the contrary, if we only see the latter, we would distort Deng Xiaoping theory or even consider it as deviation from Mao Zedong thought or Marxism. Neither affirmation nor denial of such deviation meets with reality. The key is to follow the Marxist principle of "being practical and realistic" and the dialectical, historical and material viewpoint, and objectively look at inheritance and development of practice and theory. If we cannot hold onto a dialectical view of development, we would create abstract identity theory or dualism which splits history. The way we evaluate the relationship between Deng Xiaoping theory and Mao Zedong thought is exactly how we evaluate the relationship between Mao Zedong thought and Marxism. We should see both the relation and development, and both similarities and differences.

Under new historical conditions, Mr. Deng Xiaoping objectively analyzed the social and historical situation with the basic principle of historical materialism, correctly determined the social and historical orientation of our country, put forward the pathway, guidelines and policies for the beginning stage of socialism, and started a new stage of socialist modernization construction. It was a pathway which combines theory and practice, and ideal and reality. By walking on the pathway, China eventually "got rich" following the achievement of "standing up" in Mao Zedong period. It was a great contribution to Chinese nation, socialism, and humanity's advancement. Deng Xiaoping theory is the 2nd historical leap of Marxism's Sinicization. Mr. Deng Xiaoping resolutely held onto the four basic principles, the guiding position of Marxism and Mao Zedong thought to ensure socialist direction of China's opening and reform, and avoid the tragedy of Soviet Union's collapse. Under his leadership, China rolled out its socialist construction, made miraculous achievements in a short period of 40 years, "got rich", and gradually approached the center of world stage.

Socialism with Chinese characteristics was a practical choice based on reflections on traditional and classic socialism. Compared with the "socialism" and "communism" put forward by the author of Marxism, it was still unqualified. As a result, some people, on the standpoint of traditional socialism and mature socialism depicted by classic writers, criticize socialism with Chinese characteristics and even the opening and reform, and believe that socialism with Chinese characteristics and the opening and reform have deviated from scientific socialism's principles and pushed China closer and closer to capitalism. These people could not see the huge progress we made or the leap from poverty to abundance after opening and reform. Without distinguishing the primary and secondary, and exaggerating problems and contradictions in reality, they criticize reality with abstract and ideal principles, and even deny the opening and reform by quoting the first 30 years' achievements. They neglect, or fail to look at socialism with Chinese characteristics as a sinicized form, and China's opening and reform is conducted under Marxist guidance. By severing up the internal relation between socialism with Chinese characteristics and Marxism, they are denying the merits of Marxism in China's progress to become a rich country. Since they could not see the difference between socialism with Chinese characteristics and classic socialism, they have neglected the special contribution of socialism with Chinese characteristics.

The process China "stood up" and "got rich" is exactly the history of Marxism's Sinicization, and the history

Chinese Communists rejuvenated the nation by using Marxism. History has strongly proved that China has "stood up" and "got rich" under Marxist guidance. Today, China is stepping into a period of "getting strong", and Marxist guidance is really needed in this period. From a Marxist standpoint, viewpoint and methodology, we should properly understand the relationship between revolution, construction and reform, and the dialectical relation between "standing up", "getting rich" and "getting strong". By adhering to Marxist guidance, we can analyze the reality and situation of the world, nation and Party from a historical materialist standpoint, viewpoint and methodology, guide our practice with latest result of Marxism's Sinicization, organically combine national rejuvenation and the construction of a community of shared future for mankind, and make greater contribution for people's interests and human's progress.

II

As we pointed out already, we need to start with the social and historical transformations in modern times in China, explain Marxism's social and historical significance in Chinese revolution, construction and reforms, and explain how it led Chinese people to "stand up" and "get rich" in order to comprehend the relationship between Marxism and China. Under the guidance of Marxism, Chinese people stepped out of the trap of repeated defeat, saw the light through clouds, overthrew the three big mountains, founded the People's Republic of China, and accomplished the first theoretical leap of Marxism's Sinicization -- Mao Zedong thought. Similarly, under the guidance of "liberating thoughts and being practical and realistic" as well as Marxism, China became a rich country by walking the path of socialism with Chinese characteristics. Thus, the second theoretical leap was accomplished by giving birth to the theory of socialism with Chinese characteristics. Based on the great achievements of socialist construction, the Party made an important historical judgment in the 19th National Congress. On the journey of national rejuvenation, Chinese people progressed from the stage of "getting rich" to the stage of "getting strong", and Chinese society entered a new period of development. As clearly pointed out in the 19th National Congress: "After a long-term struggle, socialism with Chinese characteristics has progressed into new times, and this is our new historical orientation for development." It was an important judgment on reality and development orientation. Then, do we still need Marxist guidance in the process of "getting strong"? How do we analyze our social and historical orientation with Marxist theory? In what aspect shall we adhere to Marxist guidance? We can easily have vague or wrong understandings in these fundamental issues. With the comprehensive development of Chinese society and economy, the theoretical and practical significance of Marxism faded out in some people's minds. It was like a "outdoors" god or "suspended" concept which can be easily removed. Properly understanding the guiding position of Marxism in new times is the key to understanding the relationship between Marxism and modern China. By resolutely following Marxism as the guiding principle, China would have an internal spirit and theoretical guarantee in its process of "getting strong".

We have a new subject followed by new theories in the new times. As pointed out in the Party's 19th National Congress: "Since the 18th NC, the domestic and overseas situation and the development of our causes posed an important subject to us. We must answer questions theoretically and practically, such as what kind of socialism with Chinese characteristics we should follow and develop, and how to follow and develop socialism with Chinese characteristics... Centered on this important subject of the times... We created the socialism with Chinese characteristics in the new times." Our Party "adheres to dialectical materialism and historical materials, integrates conditions of the times and practical requirements, and with a new vision, deepen our understandings on the Communist Party's ruling principles, construction principles of socialism and principles of human society development. It carried out arduous theoretical explorations, made great theoretical innovations, and created the socialism with Chinese characteristics in the new times." The socialism with Chinese characteristics in Xi Jinping's times is the latest result of Marxism's Sinicization and the practical guideline we must follow in the long run when we try to "get strong" and realize the dream of national rejuvenation. To be precise, following Marxism means to affirm the guiding position of Marxism in our journey of "getting strong", and the guiding position of socialism with Chinese characteristics in Xi Jinping's times in the long run.

History has strongly proved that Marxism was a scientific theory for Chinese people, and it ignited Chinese people's subjective spirit to change their fate and create history. The combination of Marxism with China's practice changed modern Chinese history. As a result, Chinese people "stood up" and "became rich". The guiding position of Marxism in revolution, construction and reforms and its contribution to our national rejuvenation is an undeniable historical fact. However, with the improvement of China's international standing and the coming of new times, do we still need to follow Marxism as the guiding principle? And how to adhere to the guiding position of Marxism?

In what aspects Marxism is still our strong weapon on the road ahead? These are important and fundamental questions we are faced with. To properly answer these questions, we should understand the relationship between socialism with Chinese characteristics in Xi Jinping's times and Marxism, the position of Marxism in socialist construction, and remove our vague or wrong understandings. Today, the key to understanding the practical role of Marxism in modern China is to understand whether we should adhere to, and how to adhere to the guiding position of Marxism when we "get strong".

Although the central government has repeated emphasized, and took strong measures to strengthen the guiding position of Marxism, there is still the trend of thought in society which denies Marxism's guiding position and criticizes CCP's leadership. They deny Marxism's guiding role for Chinese society and the scientific nature of Marxism itself. Along with improvement of our global standing, increase of comprehensive strength, and development of social economy, and especially, when we have set up and improved our socialist market economy system, new viewpoints in denial of Marxism appeared. People holding such viewpoints do not deny Marxist theory in general or deny Marxism's important role in Chinese revolution, construction and reform. According to their viewpoints, since China has "got strong" and developed its social economy, Marxism is becoming insignificant and unfit for the times and the practice of China. They deny Marxism's role in guiding the future, and believe that Marxism does not work anymore. China has become rich and strong, and no longer requires revolution or criticism against exploitation and suppression. They suggest that China needs new thoughts and theories in the new times, and may create its own theories; or they say we can take Marxism lightly, not for real, otherwise we would harm ourselves and others. In one word, they are advising us to abandon Marxism indirectly or directly. Their viewpoints are a new version of "outdatedness theory". On the basis of change of times, uniqueness of new times, or thought innovation, their theories have attracted the masses and produced wide influence in a hidden and gradual manner.

In fact, the outdatedness theory has existed for a long time. Many foreign theorists generally hold such standings when they criticize Marx, such as Habermas' late capitalism, Giddens' critique of modernity, and Baudrillard's consumer society. By resorting to new changes of western capitalist society, they emphasize historical breakage, and criticize the outdatedness of Marxist capital criticism theory and Marxism's failure in surpassing modernity. These viewpoints can be challenged theoretically, however; as Marx himself said that capital can change in the form but not in principle. Social change in modern society is within the boundaries of capital principle and has not jumped out of the scope of Marx' criticism. As Sartre said, as long as the modern social conditions criticized by Marx still remain, Marxism will remain as an undefeated philosophy. Great thoughts can penetrate history, and Marxism is one of these thoughts. It has provided not only abstract doctrines, but methodology to understand and solve problems. Therefore, we cannot doubt the scientificity and reasonability of the entire theory on the basis of historical change. Maybe some assertions in Marxism are restricted by history and became outdated, the entire thought system and spiritual principle of Marxism still carry strong explanatory capability and vital force. Now we are still living in the social and historical conditions criticized by Marxism. Besides, Marxist theory does not only include criticism against capitalism, but basic principles on the level of worldview and imagination of future society. When we are becoming strong, our adherence to Marxist guidance is not limited to specific conclusions and propositions of Marxism; instead, we should use Marxist standpoints, viewpoints and methodology based on China's social and historical orientation, and creatively follow and develop Marxism.

While explaining that China is walking into a new era, the Party's report in 19th National Congress pointed out: "The change of major contradictions of our society has not changed our judgment that we are in the beginning stage of socialism, and we are still the largest developing country in the world." The new era continues with the past and opens up the future. New thoughts guiding the new era are keeping abreast of Mao Zedong thought and Deng Xiaoping theory, which are sinicized form of Marxism, and they are the development and application of Marxism. After "getting strong", China will continue to follow and develop Marxism. It is very important to dialectically understand the relationship between socialism with Chinese characteristics in Xi Jinping's times, Marxism and sinicized Marxism from a historical materialist point of view. Only by adhering to Marxism can we properly understand modern China's historical orientation and development direction for future, and make greater contribution to national rejuvenation and humanity's progress.

The Party's 19th NC report made an important judgment on China's social and historical orientation that China has entered a new era of "getting strong". This judgment will have profound influence on China's development in future and world history development. While we are discussing the relationship between Marxism and modern China today, we should, in fact, discuss Marxism's role in rejuvenation of Chinese nation and the relationship between Marxism and socialist with Chinese characteristics in the Xi Jinping's times. For today's China, adhering to Marxism means to adhere to Marxism's guiding position in our great practice to "get strong", use

Marxist methodology to analyze China's social reality and guide modern China's construction; and in the meantime, develop and improve Marxism in our practice.

The important judgment that China has entered a new era of "getting strong" was made by analyzing China's reality with historical materialist methodology. Since the opening and reform, our country made great changes in politics and economy, achieved moderate prosperity, and will remove poverty nationwide in two years. It can be said that 40 years' opening and reform enabled China to develop rapidly and make achievements which western developed countries took decades or a hundred years to make; consequently, Chinese society has acquired a completely new outlook. How to understand the reality of modern Chinese society and determine its historical orientation is the basis for our decision-making. Today, Chinese society's major contradiction has changed from the contradiction between people's growing need for material and culture and the backward social production to the contradiction between people's growing need for happy life and unbalanced and insufficient development. It was an important political judgment President Xi Jinping made on behalf of the Party. Based on above judgment, we know that China has entered a new era of "getting strong". Major contradiction of society changed, so the society manifests the basic signs of stage change. It is the basic viewpoint of historical materialism. In the preface to *Critique of Political Economy,* Marx pointed out: "We cannot judge a person based on his own judgment; similarly, we cannot judge a changing era based on awareness; instead, we must explain such awareness by diving into contradictions in material life and the conflicts between productive force and productive relations." The judgment that China is walking into a new era was made based on the change of major contradictions of Chinese society, and was a scientific judgment consistent with China's social reality. After 40 years' development, our country basically got rid of the state of material shortage, poverty and backwardness; people's material and cultural life was enriched, and there is growing need for a happy life above the level of material and culture. Our new target is to fulfill the people's living requirements on all sides. Solving the contradiction between people's growing need for a happy life and unbalanced and insufficient development has become the basic task in the new times.

Faced with new changes of major contradiction, Chinese society went into a new era of "getting strong". The Party's 19th NC report explained the nature and connotation of the new era: "Socialism with Chinese characteristics has entered a new era, and such an advancement will play an important role in the history of the People's Republic of China, Chinese nation, world socialism and human society." The Party's 19th NC report explained such a role with "three indications", and stated that such an advancement "indicates that Chinese nation, which endured great difficulty in the past, has now achieved the great leap from standing up, getting rich to getting strong, and the bright future of national rejuvenation is ahead of us. It indicates that scientific socialism is displaying strong vitality in China in the 21st century, and the great flag of socialism with Chinese characteristics has been raised high in the world. It also indicates that the pathway, theory, system and culture of socialism with Chinese characteristics are developing continuously.

They opened up new pathways to modernity for developing countries, provided a new choice for countries and nations which wished to accelerate their development while maintaining their independence, and contributed Chinese wisdom and program for the solution of humanity's problems." From a dual prospective of national country and world history, the Party's 19th NC report explained the significance of socialism with Chinese characteristics walking into the new era, connected the great rejuvenation of Chinese nation with socialism's development and humanity's progress, and fully reflected Marxism's viewpoint, standpoint and methodology. As emphasized in the report: "The new era is a period which we shall inherit the past and look into the future, continue to gain victory in socialist construction under new historical conditions, build a moderately prosperous society and a socialist, modern and strong country, unite all nations to create a happy life and accomplish common prosperity, work together to realize the dream of national rejuvenation, and enable our country to walk into the center of world stage and make great contribution to humanity." The report explained the basic meaning and significance of the new era with grand words, revealed the historical orientation of the new era; therefore it is a historical materialist explanation and understanding of China's reality.

The new era of socialism with Chinese characteristics is the era in which Chinese nation rejuvenates itself and went from the stage of "getting rich" to "getting strong", and in which we are building a socialist, modern and strong country under the guidance of socialism with Chinese characteristics. The Party's 19th NC report made a strategic plan of "two steps" for the development in the new era; and for achieving "two 100 years" in stages. "In the first stage, or 2020-2035, we will work hard for another 15 years based on our success in building a moderately prosperous society in order to achieve socialist modernization on the whole." "In the second stage, or 2035-middle of century, we will work hard for another 15 years based on our success in basic modernization in order to build a socialist, modernized and strong country of prosperity, democracy, civilization, harmony and beauty." Prosperity, democracy, civilization, harmony and beauty are the basic requirements for a socialist, modernized and strong country, and basic targets for

China to "get strong" in the new era. The five keywords summarized our objectives in the aspects of economy, politics, culture, society and environment. A "strong" country is not only strong in economy and military, but means comprehensive advancement and development of society, and the process of general change. "Getting strong" is not the rising of a new country, but the great rejuvenation of Chinese nation, and a process in which Marxism is combined with creative development of traditional Chinese culture in order to explore new forms and living modes of human civilization and walk into the future. Therefore, "getting strong" is a process in which we push forward human advancement by rejuvenating the Chinese nation.

The new times give birth to, and require new thoughts. It is an era which requires and has produced new thoughts. Socialism with Chinese characteristics in Xi Jinping's times is a flag guiding us to "get strong". The thought is the latest result of Marxism's Sinicization and the theoretical fruit created based on change of major contradiction in Chinese society. Just as the new era is an era when we learn from the past and look into the future, new thoughts also have similar characteristics. They are the succession and development of sinicized Marxism, and new forms of Chinese Marxism in 21st century. The Party's 19th NC report clearly pointed out: "Socialism with Chinese characteristics in new times is the succession and development of Marxism-Leninism, Mao Zedong thought, Deng Xiaoping theory, 'three represents' and scientific outlook on development, the latest result of Marxism's Sinicization, the fruit of practical experience and group wisdom of the Party and the people, an important component of the theory system of socialism with Chinese characteristics, and a practical guideline for our Party and people to realize great rejuvenation of Chinese nation. It must be held onto and developed in the long run." Organically combining Marxism with modern China's conditions, practical targets and development strategies, and adhering to the guiding position of Marxism during socialist construction aiming at "getting strong" is the prominent characteristic of socialism with Chinese characteristics in Xi Jinping's times.

Modern China's pathway of development is a pathway of Marxism's Sinicization, and a sinicized pathway on which Marxist theory is combined with China's practice. On one hand, we adhere to Marxism's guiding position; on the other, we keep innovating and developing Marxism in our practice. A theory must keep pace with the times to become a leading theory. Socialist construction with Chinese characteristics is inseparable from Marxist guidance, and it pushed Marxism to new heights in history. The key is to follow and develop Marxism based on practice and be a successor and innovator instead of a doctrinaire who holds onto remnants. We adhere to Marxism not based on doctrines, but with reflections and succession. It was criticism against tradition, and development therefrom opened up our socialist pathway with Chinese characteristics, and created socialist thoughts with Chinese characteristics. In the new era when China is "getting strong", we need to follow and develop Marxism by considering our development in the times. Our book will explain Marxism's guiding role for China's construction in 7 aspects. On this basis and in the final part, we will explain the role of a strong China for innovation and development of Marxism itself.

Firstly, we should adhere to the guidance of Marxist political party theory. CCP is the backbone for national rejuvenation, and its leadership is the core of socialism with Chinese characteristics. CCP and China's political party system are fundamentally different from the political parties and political party system of western countries. CCP is a political party armed with Marxist theory and grew up in the revolution era, and the only governing party leading China's socialist construction. Our country has adopted the system of multi-party cooperation and political consultation under CCP's leadership. Adhering to Marxist political party theory, following and improving the Party's leadership, and pushing forward Party construction is the fundamental guarantee for rejuvenation of Chinese nation. "History has proved, and will continue to prove that national rejuvenation is only a fantasy without the Party's leadership." To follow and improve the Party's leadership, we must follow Marxist political party theory and improve the theory in practice. Without the guidance of Marxist political party theory, we will lose our fighting capacity in front of modern multi-party system and democracy, and will lose our direction in front of anarchism and de-organization.

Secondly, we should adhere to people's principal position theory in Marxism. The great rejuvenation of Chinese nation and the construction of a socialist, modernized and strong country is the common will and cause of all Chinese people, and cannot be independently completed by any one political party or class. Therefore, we must gather the people's effort and wisdom, protect their democratic rights, ignite their pioneering spirit, call for their participation, and create a strong force to construct a socialist, modernized and strong country. We must adhere to Marxist historical view which emphasizes the people's role in creating history, properly handle the dialectical relation between leaders, political party and the people, and organically integrate the Party's leadership, the people's participation and governance according to law. In Marxism, the people's principal position means that we should "adhere to the pathway of socialism with Chinese characteristics, adhere to and improve the system of people's congress, multi-party cooperation and political consultation under CCP's leadership, regional ethnic autonomy and self-governance at community level, strengthen and develop the broadest patriotic united front, develop socialist consultative democracy, improve democratic system, enrich democratic forms, expand democratic channels, and ensure people's principal position in the country's political life and social life." We should not only protect the people's democratic rights, but awaken their innovative spirit and satisfy their basic interests in order to increase their enthusiasm, enhance their national pride, ignite their patriotic passion, and encourage their participation in construction of this socialist, modernized and strong country and national rejuvenation.

Thirdly, we should adhere to the ideological theory of Marxism. Marxism is the guiding thought of socialism with Chinese characteristics and is guiding China on all sides in the new times, including the practical and theoretical aspects. With the emergence of self-media and multi-media, public thoughts and opinions are diversified and complicated and have stronger and stronger influence. China, as a strong country, is in a complex ideological environment. In ideological construction, it is very important to adhere to Marxism's guiding position. Meanwhile, with the increase of China's hard power, China's growth will require and be reflected in the proactive construction of Chinese discourse, theory, thoughts and spirit. As a result, ideological and theoretical construction is becoming an urgent affair. The guidance of Marxist ideological theory, innovation of ideological working pattern, and working with a brain armed with Marxist theory is the necessary requirement in the new era of increased strength.

Fourthly, we should adhere to the modernity criticism theory in Marxism. A fundamental issue of how to face modernity exists in China's history of modern times and how it rejuvenated itself and "got strong". In the core, it was an attitude towards modernity which determines different views of thought trends and social strengths on China's development path and direction. To deny modernity with cultural conservatism, surpass it with radicalism, embrace it with affirmation, or create a dialectical standing unifying criticism and surpassing is of crucial importance for our pathway in socialist construction and the rejuvenation of our civilization for "getting strong". In this issue, the standing of criticism must be held onto as a dialectical part of Marxism. Marx is a thinker who created a systematic modernity criticism theory. He is both a successor and critic of modernity. Draining nutrition from Marx' modernity criticism theory and adhering to its dialectical standing is exactly our difference from traditional socialism and capitalism. Rejuvenation of Chinese nation has contained a predictive direction where Marxism will surpass modern capitalist civilization, but the positive results of modernity must be used to criticize certain aspects of tradition. Socialism with Chinese characteristics, and especially, the "Chinese characteristics" was named as such because the dialectical critic standing was held onto in the social context consisting of pre-modern, modern and post-modern factors.

Fifthly, we should adhere to world history theory in Marxism. China in strength, is a country which rejuvenates itself and pushes forward humanity's advancement, and which should play a role in such businesses, oppose to unreasonable international political and economic order, and set up new international relations. Therefore, China in strength needs real great power diplomacy and should establish great power diplomatic principles and strategies, surpass modern international relation theory, create international relation and diplomatic theory with Chinese characteristics, and make contribution to world peace and humanity's advancement. In diplomatic relations, China should break through the hegemonic principles arising in modern times, oppose to all forms of power politics and old and new colonialism, and embrace the principles of equality, mutual benefit and peace. We should not only adhere to Marxism's guiding position, but, under the guidance of world history theory, globalization theory, and war and peace theory of Marxism, make effort to create a better international environment for our rejuvenation and contribute to the creation of a community of shared future for mankind and humanity's advancement.

Sixthly, we must adhere to the communism theory in Marxism. CCP formulated its own guidelines in the beginning of foundation, consisting of the lowest guideline and highest guideline. These are action principles for our work from achieving national independence, democracy and prosperity to gradually realizing our great dram of communism. CCP's guidelines have combined reality with ideals, incorporating short-term tasks and humanity's dream. Now, when we are working toward the goal of national rejuvenation, we also need to combine reality and ideals and hold onto communism theory in Marxism. If we do not have a great dream and direction surpassing modern civilization, our rejuvenation will not play an important role in world history.

Seventhly, we should adhere to Marxist methodology. During the process of Chinese revolution, construction and reforms, CCP has been emphasizing Marxism's Sinicization, and how to guide practice in real life with sinicized Marxism. And during the process of Marxism's Sinicization, the Marxist methodology and worldview are used to guide China's practice. Sinicization means to analyze China's practice with Marxist standpoints, viewpoints and methods instead of copying all contents and conclusions of Marxism. In the new era of "getting strong", it carries great significance to adhere to the basic methodology and thinking mode in Marxism.

Finally, after explaining, in 7 aspects, that China in strength must follow the guidance of Marxism in its socialist practice with Chinese characteristics, we will explain with one chapter's length new development of Marxism during such practice. There is always a dialectical relationship between succession and innovation and between adherence and development. Sinicized Marxism is not a doctrine book. China's Marxists always combine Marxism with China's reality, develop Marxism while adhering to it, create Marxist theory with Chinese characteristics and keep on enriching and developing such theory. In our revolution and construction, we created Mao Zedong thought and led the country to "stand up". In opening and reform, we created Deng Xiaoping theory and achieved the goal of "getting rich". Today, socialism with Chinese characteristics has entered a new era of "getting strong". China has walked into a new era when the primary task is to construct a socialist, modernized and strong country, and when socialism with Chinese characteristics centered on Xi Jinping was created. Socialism with Chinese characteristics centered on Xi Jinping is the latest result of Marxism's Sinicization, and Chinese Marxism in the 21st century. It lifted Marxism to a new historical height and understanding, and while adhering to Marxism, it also represents

Marxism's development. The theory and practice of socialism with Chinese characteristics in the new times is enriching and developing socialism and Marxism, and providing them with rich national contents and modern characteristics.

III

Undeniably, China has "stood up" and "got rich" under CCP's leadership. Then, does China still need CCP's leadership in the process of getting stronger? The Party's 19th National Congress set out a grand purpose of strengthening China; and meanwhile, of adhering to and maintaining CCP's leadership. "Among the Party, political circle, military, civilians and students, the Party is the leader" is not only a general political viewpoint or slogan, but carries political connotation and implication consistent with our purpose of "getting strong". We should have a solid understanding that CCP's leadership is essential in our effort to "get strong". Under CCP's leadership, we will learn from history, analyze reality, and follow the proper theory. Marxism, especially the Marxist political party theory, is the proper theory. CCP's leadership is as important to China as is Marxism.

President Xi Jinping pointed out that socialism with Chinese characteristics has entered a new era, and that we are closer to, and have more confidence and capacity in realizing the goal of national rejuvenation than any period in history. Then, why do we, in such a period, emphasize adhering to and maintaining CCP's leadership? It has been determined by the objective reality faced by socialism with Chinese characteristics in the new times.

Firstly, we are experiencing an unprecedented situation in width and depth of development, complexity of interest relations, and intensity of power struggles in the new times. We need to carry on great struggles with many new historical characteristics. People around the country must be united, and this can only be carried out under CCP's leadership. The Party's 19th NC report set out new targets of national rejuvenation, but these targets cannot be easily achieved with little effort. We must organize talks, coordinate interests, sort out relations and unite the Party and people's heart. What kind of power, apart from CCP in modern China, could fulfill such a mission? Chinese people have realized with insight that only a hardworking and united nation has a future and hope. For a nation, unity is its source of power and victory. Chinese people suffered a lot due to its disunity and scattering state. It was not until birth of CCP when China went from disunity to unity, fragmentation to wholeness, and timidity to strength. Today, China really need CCP as the core part of strength to unite the entire nation and country. CCP has demonstrated unparalleled capability of mobilizing the people, and is able to draw the largest concentric circle gathering force on all sides.

Secondly, when socialism with Chinese characteristics is entering a new era, the question becomes urgent and prominent that how to ensure people's interest as topmost priority and people's principal position. A political force will ensure the people's principal position, serve the people wholeheartedly and be supported and admired by the people only when it "centers on the people", regards people as creators of history and fundamental force determining the national fate and future. In today's China, such a political force is no other than CCP. A political party's class nature is in who it represents, and CCP represents the people. Representation of the people is one of the major characteristics of socialism with Chinese characteristics in the new times. "People" is the most frequently used word with 203 appearances in the 19th NC report. In the beginning of the report, President Xi Jinping pointed out: "Keep our initial intention to fulfill our mission. The initial intention and mission of Chinese Communists is to provide happiness for Chinese people and rejuvenation for the nation." In the part "Thoughts and Basic Strategies of Socialism with Chinese Characteristics in the New Times", President Xi Jinping explained centeredness on people, people's principal position, people's comprehensive development, people's common prosperity, people's leading role and improvement of people's livelihood in thoughts of socialism with Chinese characteristics in the new times. The leadership of such a Party deeply connected with the people will provide continuous momentum for great rejuvenation of Chinese nation.

Thirdly, when socialism with Chinese characteristics has entered a new era, the political force leading people on this pathway will be faced with major risks and tests. The political party bearing such a historical mission will provide solid guarantee for its cause only when it implements discipline, and with strong willpower, fight corruption, eliminate potential risks within, renew internal political atmosphere and keep improving its political ecology. Obviously, only CCP is equipped with such conditions. Since the 18th NC, we made great achievements in Party's self-governance. And the 19th NC report emphasized that self-governance is always alongside, and that our Party is faced with long-term and complex tests in governance, opening and reform, market economy and external environment. It put forward general requirements for Party construction in the new times, emphasizing that the Party's political construction is the top priority, and strengthening ideal belief is the primary task in thought construction. The report also set out measures to construct a high-quality cadre team and strengthen grass-root organization construction. The Party's 19th NC report showed a solid determination that "we will gain overwhelming victory in anti-corruption", and used grand, powerful words such as "no hidden zone", "full coverage", "zero tolerance", "strengthening threat to conquer corruption", "tighten the cage of anti-corruption", "enhance awareness of anti-corruption". People will certainly put trust in such a political party which "makes continuous efforts to build a system of clean hands."

Fourthly, the progress of socialism with Chinese characteristics into the new era indicates that Chinese nation accomplished the great leap from "standing up" and "getting rich" to "getting strong". A political party in the leading position must use its discretion of times and trends, lead people to welcome and adapt to the new times, and put forth new targets and directions based on the strength requirements of the new times in order to enjoy a bright future with the people. This is what CCP is working on. In the Party's 19th NC report, President Xi Jinping made an important political judgment that "after long-term effort, China entered a new era in construction of socialism with Chinese characteristics, and this is a new historical orientation for our development." The new historical orientation was built on change of major contradiction of our society. Xi Jinping pointed out in the report: "Major contradiction of our society has turned into the contradiction between people's growing need for a happy life and unbalanced and insufficient development." It was indeed a correct conclusion based on history and reality, theory and practice, and thoughts in aspects of domestic and global conditions. President Xi Jinping's discussion that socialism with Chinese characteristics has entered a new era and Chinese society's major contradiction has turned into "contradiction between people's growing need for a happy life and unbalanced and insufficient development", and his promise that CCP must strive hard to satisfy people's need for a happy life have won the ardent attention and wide support of Chinese people. In this situation, the people understand that their need for "material and culture" and for "democracy, legal governance, fairness, justice, safety and environment" can be met by following the Party's leadership. In this way, they will accomplish "free and comprehensive development", create a new mode of existence for humans and walk into a new civilization. CCP representing the direction of historical advancement will certainly win the admiration and support of the people.

The Communist Manifesto is the first guideline of Communist Party as a proletarian party. In *The Communist Manifesto*, Marx and Engels explained in depth why we should found a proletarian political party and the nature and purpose of Communist Party.

Marx and Engels asserted: "Among all classes standing in opposition to capitalist class, only the proletarian class is truly revolutionary." The reason is that proletarian class is the product of modern large-scale industry and represents advanced productive force and the society's future. "Among all productive tools, the strongest is the revolutionary class itself." The proletarian class represents the most advanced productive force, and it has become "the strongest productive force" itself. The proletarian class is "the slave of capitalist countries" situated at the "bottom of society". For this class, there is nothing to keep, and they will be liberated only by destroying everything protecting private property and enabling common sharing by society.

The proletarian class is the most revolutionary, and called the "gravedigger" of capitalism as the bearer of the mission to overthrow capitalism and set up a new society. How does it fulfill this historical mission? Marx and Engels pointed out that the proletarian class must set up a proletarian revolutionary party, or Communist

Party in order to fulfill its historical mission. They also emphasized that Communist Party is the leading force of revolution, and its correct leadership is the basic guarantee for proletarian mission. Marx and Engels said: "Proletariat's organization as a class, and then a political party has always been damaged by competition among workers, but such organizations always regenerate, and with increasing force, solidity and strength."

In the beginning of the 2nd part of *The Communist Manifesto*, the following question was raised up: "What is the relationship between Communists and the entire proletariat?" Marx and Engels answered that Communists is not a special political part standing in competition against other workers' political parties, and does not have any interest different from those of the proletarian class. "They don't propose any special principles to shape the proletariat's movement." In other words, the Communist Party, in nature, fully represents the proletarian class' interests, and the Communists are fully dedicated to the proletarian class' interests. Apart from loyally representing the proletarian class' interests, the Communist Party has no "special interest". If the Communist Party has any "private interest" besides proletarian class' interests, it will change its nature into a party other than a proletarian party. Since the proletarian class' interests are highly consistent with those of the people, representing their interests means to represent the people's interests.

Marx and Engels have summarized the major characteristics of Communists in theory and practice: "In practice, Communists are the most determined and pioneering among all workers' political parties. In theory, they win over other proletarian people because they understand the conditions, process and general result of proletarian movement." In other words, the Communist Party is an organization which always joins proletarian revolution with solid actions and determination, understands deeply under which conditions a proletarian revolutionary movement is created, how it proceeds, and what kind of result it will finally produce.

CCP is a proletarian political party, and according to Marx and Engels' discussion on the nature of proletarian political parties, CCP's purpose is to loyally represent the interests of the proletarian class and laboring people, and be dedicated for the above interests. With this purpose, CCP led Chinese people to "stand up" and "get rich", and will continue to lead Chinese people to "get strong".

CCP's legitimacy in leading Chinese people is in its foundation set up in people's interests. President Xi Jinping made amazing achievements in country governance and won applause around the world as a major leader of the Party and country, because he has profound understanding that legitimacy of governance is whether the Party is governing "for the people", and he is effectively practicing this concept. He put forward the conclusion that "people's support is the greatest politics", which has briefly stated CCP's legitimacy of governance. "People's support", as he said, "carries wholeness in theory, practice, and history", and "connotations in people's livelihood and democracy". "In other words, 'people's support' is won by the Party's solid effort to fight corruption and improve people's livelihood. Both aspects are combined in an organic unity." On a historical materialist height, he mentioned that as a Marxist governing Party, CCP'a greatest political advantage is to connect with the people closely, and the greatest danger is separation from the people. In his speech in a face-to-face meeting between members of the Standing Committee of the 18th Political Bureau and Chinese and foreign journalists, or the 1st formal speech after he assumed office as the president, he declared: "People's aspiration for a happy life is our work target." He said, "I received this relay baton of history to work hard for great rejuvenation of Chinese nation, enable Chinese nation to stand strongly among all nations of the world, and make greater contribution to humanity". This is a major responsibility. "This major responsibility is responsibility for the people." He said, "Our people love life and expect good education, steady jobs, satisfactory income, reliable social assurance, high-level medical services, comfortable living conditions, beautiful environment, and healthy growth, good jobs and good life of children." "People's aspiration for good life is our work target." He promised to the entire Party and the people: "I will mutual affinity with the people, work with them, struggle with them, work hard in my office, and hand in a qualified answer sheet to history and the people." In the Party's 19th NC report, he quoted "centeredness on people" as the basic strategy for adhering to and developing socialism with Chinese characteristics in the new times. After 5 years, people have seen that the Party Central Committee centered on Xi Jinping "handed in a satisfactory answer sheet to the people" and assumed the "major responsibility" of realizing "people's aspiration for a happy life". Correspondingly, the people admire and recognize CCP's leadership, and legitimacy of CCP's governance is strengthened over time. The above is the basis of CCP's legitimacy in leading people to "get strong".

While recognizing CCP's legitimacy in leading Chinese people to "get strong", we cannot be trapped in "constitutional democracy". Marx profoundly revealed the true nature of "legitimacy" of "constitutional democracy" of capitalist class. According to his viewpoint, the capitalist political system is often titled with "constitutional democracy", but such "democracy" is actually "pro-forma democracy", and the legitimacy of capitalist political system is based on maintaining "pro-forma democracy" instead of "real democracy". The "legitimacy" of capitalist "constitutional democracy" only applies to and serves capitalist production mode.

Socialist China under CCP's leadership, however, has its own standard of "legitimacy" suitable for its production mode and its own "legitimacy" resources. If socialist China introduces the standard of "legitimacy" of western "constitutional democracy" and uses it to measure its own "legitimacy", then CCP will be trapped in "constitutional democracy" in terms of "legitimacy". Due to China's social reality and nature, CCP cannot adopt western "constitutional democracy". If we copy western "constitutional democracy" while "getting strong", CCP may lose its leadership and China will not "get strong".

Marxist political party theory has also explained the relationship between the people, classes, political parties and leaders. In this aspect, Lenin had an important statement: "The people are divided by class, and only when groups are separated in social structure of production can we separate the people from classes. Generally, and on most occasions, at least in modern civilized countries, classes are led by political parties. Political parties are headed by a steady group of people who are the most prestigious, influential and experienced, selected for important positions and called 'leaders'.'" Lenin's words profoundly explained the relationship between the people, classes, political parties and leaders, and their roles in creation of history.

To easily understand the relationship between the people and classes, and between the people, classes and political parties, we must understand the relationship between the people, classes, political parties and leaders. To accomplish their great historical mission, the people and proletarian class should have their own political parties and leaders. The needs for political parties and for leaders are consistent. If the people and proletarian class do not have their own political parties, they are actually trying to sail to the ideal land without a boat. And if they do not have their own leaders, they are lacking a steersman on their boat. In other words, the people and proletarian class need a leader with "the most prestige, influence and experience" because they need a steersman to control direction and ride through waves in their journey to the other land of beauty. As to the absolute necessity of leaders, Marx said: "As Claude Arien Helv étius said, every social period has its own heroes, and if there is not, it will create heroes." Lenin was more straightforward on this matter: "According to history, if a class cannot elect its political leaders and advanced representatives who are good at organizing and leading movements, they will not be able to govern the country." "Training a group of experienced and prestigious Party leaders is a long-term and arduous task, but if we do not carry it out, proletarian dictatorship and 'unity of thought' will remain in words only."

According to Marxist political party theory, the leaders of the people and proletarian class are playing an important role because they don't have special personal interests and can represent the noble character and selflessness of proletarian class; on the other hand, as revolutionists and thinkers, they can solve complex problems in theory, and lead the Party, classes and the people to carry out struggles in practice. They embody tight unity of theory and practice. Engels described how Marx became a leader of proletarian class and the people: "We don't have anyone like Marx who are farseeing, and always makes the correct decision in moments requiring swift action, and his solutions are always quick and to the point." "What perturbs those insignificant, self-glorifying, complaining and mean people is that Marx won his position with his attainments in theory and practice, and even the most excellent people in workers' movements fully trust him. They seek consultation with him at critical moments, and always find that his advice is the best. He already won the position in Germany, France and Russia, not to mention smaller countries. Therefore, Marx is not imposing his opinions or will on people, but the people are seeking his advice. Marx' special and important influence on movements is based on the above foundation."

Marxist political party theory's affirmation of leaders is based on the viewpoint of historical materialism on the people and individuals' role in history. Firstly, historical materialism asserts that social existence determines social awareness, and affirms people's decisive effect in creating history. In both theory and practice, historical materialism criticizes and overcomes historical viewpoint of heroes, and regards the people as self-aware creators of history. According to historical materialism, the people are not only creators of material and spiritual wealth, but decisive force of social reforms. Mao Zedong had the following classic words on historical materialism in terms of the people being creators of history: "People, and only people are the force creating world history." Secondly, while affirming people as creators of history, historical materialism also admits individuals' role, and sometimes important role, in influencing social development. According to historical materialism, history consists of activities of different individuals. Everybody leaves some trace in history and plays certain role in his lifespan. As persons involved and initiators of historical events, historical figures left their imprints in history.

Marxist political party theory's dialectical explanation of the people and individuals' role in history has led to a dialectical analysis on the relationship between leaders and the people. On one hand, we must realize that leaders' power is provided by the people, and leaders work through people's practice. Without active participation of the people, the leaders' thoughts, no matter how correct they are, cannot be put into practice, therefore leaders must rely on the people. On the other hand, the people do need leaders. Without leaders, the people will become scattered sands in an unorganized state. Without leaders' direction and organization, the people cannot realize their beautiful dreams.

When the people understand that proletarian class and laboring masses need not only their own political party but also their own leaders, they will consciously support and admire their leaders. In this sense, support for the people's leaders is supporting the interests of the Party, classes and the people. Support and admiration for leaders are the class' self-aware act out of concerns about the people's basic interests. In 1956, Deng Xiaoping pointed out in *Report on Modifying the Party Constitution* in the 8th NC that "Our love and support for the leader reflects our love and support for the interests of the Party, classes and the people instead of individual deification." Support for the leader means support for the leader's authority, and cannot be construed as dictatorship. Engels opposed to dictatorship, but meanwhile, he criticized the saying of "anti-authoritarianism". He said: "It is ridiculous to consider authoritarian principles as absolutely bad and autonomous principles as absolutely good." And he vividly stated the importance of authority: "What has most clearly indicated the necessity of authority, and arbitrary authority is no other than a ship sailing on the vast ocean. In the critical moment, whether the people's lives can be rescued depends on whether they can obey one person's will." And he harshly criticized anti-authoritarianists: "In a word, there are two cases. If the anti-authoritarianists do not know what they are saying, they are just propagating confusing thoughts. If the know, then they have betrayed proletarian movement. In both cases, they are doing their job for reactionaries."

According to Marxist political party theory, only by supporting the leader's authority can we increase the Party's fighting capacity and ensure progress of its cause. This theory has been proved by reality following the Party's 18th NC. Since the 18th NC, China's attainments on the journey of "getting strong" was made while strengthening the authority of Party Central Committee centered on Mr. Xi Jinping. Supporting the authority of Party Central Committee centered on Mr. Xi Jinping is the political guarantee for

China to "get strong". The awareness of politics, overall situation, centeredness and cooperation as put forward by Party Central Committee centered on Mr. Xi Jinping is playing a critical role in supporting authority. Among the "four awareness", awareness of centeredness and cooperation is the most fundamental and essential, and is the criteria judging awareness of politics and overall situation. Some scholars pointed out: "Setting up the core position of Xi Jinping, supporting the authority of Party Central Committee centered on Xi Jinping, and ensuring the Party is always the core leading socialist construction with Chinese characteristics are the three concentric circles and an organic unity of cores in the sense of leaders, political party and country. They are playing an important role in creating Party consensus and initiating joint action." Both history and reality have clearly proved that a stable and authoritarian group of core leaders formed based on China's national situation, governance achievements and people's happiness is an important guarantee for the Party's political function. Without such a guarantee, China cannot "get strong". In newspapers and magazines, we often see the term "critical minority", and in the historical process of "getting strong", cadre elites, especially Party leaders are playing a critical role. Therefore, the people, especially Party members must remain on the same pace with Party Central Committee and consciously support its authority.

Marxist political party theory mainly consists of two parts: One explains the nature and purpose of proletarian political parties; the other explains how a proletarian political party carries out its construction. In modern China, the first part can be used to explain why Chinese people need the leadership of CCP in order to "get strong"; and the second part can be used by CCP to construct itself and fulfill the mission of leading Chinese people to strength. Based on explanations of the nature and purpose of proletarian political parties in Marxist political party theory, CCP's leadership must be strengthened to transform China into a strong country. When this point has been made clear, we should discuss another issue: Can CCP bear this mission? Is it capable of leading Chinese people to "get strong"? It fully depends on CCP's Party construction. If CCP is able to govern itself with strict discipline, keep constructing itself and improving its governing capacity and leadership skills, and win admiration of the people as a Marxist political party, then it will always keep pace with the times, and just as it led Chinese people to "stand up" and "get rich", it will also lead Chinese people to "get strong". How does CCP construct itself? And under what guidance will it construct itself? Undoubtedly, CCP is constructing itself under the guidance of Marxism, and precisely, Marxist theory on Party construction. Marxism, and especially Marxist political party theory has fully demonstrated its significance for modern China.

Marxism includes the theory on how a proletarian political party shall construct itself. Classic authors of Marxism believed that proletarian class must have their own political party, and systematically answered the question as to what kind of party they shall construct, and how to construct such a party. Marx and Engels established the theoretical foundation for construction of a proletarian political party. Under new historical conditions, Lenin defended and developed Marxism. He not only founded a new proletarian political party -- Russian Communist Party -- and enabling it to become the first Party governing nationwide, but also explored Party construction and created a complete political party theory. Chinese Communists, with Mao Zedong as their representative combined the basic principle of Marxism with China's practice, and created Mao Zedong's Party construction theory as part of Mao Zedong thought. While enabling CCP to become the largest proletarian political party with a long-term period of governance, Chinese Communists, represented by Mao Zedong enriched and developed Marxist political party theory with a more complete form. Marxist political party theory has a rich content including political guidelines, strategies, and organizational principles and forms of proletarian political parties. To maintain revolutionary nature and purity of proletarian political parties, Marxist political party theory emphasized that proletarian political parties must use Marxism as their theoretical basis, and must set out guidelines and slogans. All people joining the Party must unconditionally accept the Party's scientific guidelines. They shall never change the Party's final purpose into an empty slogan; instead, they shall closely combine their struggle for final purpose with political actions under current conditions. Secondly, Marxist political party theory emphasized that we should keep fighting against various non-Marxist thoughts and see though anti-Marxist thought trends to increase the Party's theoretical standard. Scientific socialism is believed to be the Party's theoretical basis, and "this is not negotiable within any proletarian political party. Discussion of these issues will indicate doubt of the entire proletarian socialism." Thirdly, Marxist political party theory emphasized domestic construction within the Party to increase the Party's cohesive force and fighting capacity, and made clear that democratic centralism is the Party's basic organizational principle. In Engels' late years, he said the communist alliance "is organized fully based on democratic principles, with committees elected by vote and dismissed at any time. In this way, the path of conspirators seeking dictatorship has been blocked." Fourthly, the Party's authority and function as the core of leadership should be strengthened. According to Marxist political party theory, democracy is not in conflict with strengthened leadership and authority of the Party. Supporting the Party's leadership and authority is a guarantee for the Party's guidelines and decisions to be implemented. Fifthly, the Party's unity is particularly emphasized. Especially, the stability and unity of the central leadership group of the Party should be maintained to prevent secession. Lenin said: "Unity of the Party and the will of pioneering group of proletarian class is the basic condition for gaining victory in proletarian dictatorship." Sixth, the Party's fine style of work should be maintained. Especially, the Party shall be closely united with the people, and the people's public servants should not become "masters". "The most horrible danger of the Communist Party is separation from the people." Seventhly, supervision inside the Party is quite important. Criticism and self-criticism shall be carried out to ensure the Party's leaders are fulfilling their duties loyally. Eighth, the Party's membership should be purified. Once the proletarian political party becomes the governing party, some cheaters and destroyers will change their appearance and join the governing party. The key to solving this problem is to "purify the membership by relying on a healthy, strong and advanced class."

All of these basic principles of Marxist party construction has become guiding thoughts for CCP to govern itself strictly. The Party's 19th NC made a comprehensive plan for "strict Party governance and enhancement of Party's governance and leadership skills." The new requirements and plans put forward in the 19th NC for strict Party governance in based on Marxist political party theory, and is the vivid reflection and innovative development of the theory in modern China. The Party's 19th NC emphasizes: "strict Party governance is always on the way", "our Party must have a new look and new achievements in the new era of socialism with Chinese characteristics." When socialism with Chinese characteristics has entered a new era, the Party's construction also has entered a new phase. The Party Central Committee centered on Mr. Xi Jinping considers it a great social reform to push forward the construction of socialism with Chinese characteristics in the new times, and considers strict governance as the "self revolution" required for the success of the former.

Because there have been some corrupt individuals in CCP since opening and reform, some people doubt whether CCP is still able to correct and purify itself and lead Chinese people to "get strong". A political party is an organization founded for certain political purpose, and naturally, it does not wish to make mistakes; and the smaller the mistakes are, the better the situation will be. Suppose it does not make any mistake, it will achieve its purpose more smoothly. But according to history, it is obviously impossible for political parties, groups, organizations and political figures not to make any mistake, and Marxist political parties are not an exception. Escaping from mistakes is a sign of weakness, and Marxist political parties should face their mistakes. CCP should face its mistakes in history, including corruption at this moment. As a basic historical fact, CCP has made mistakes, but it is able to correct itself at the right time to get out of the crisis. On one hand, CCP has the thought weapon to correct mistakes; on the other hand, CCP has democratic centralism as its correction mechanism. After the 18th NC, the Party made great achievements in anti-corruption struggle which revealed the severity of corruption problem, but at the root, it is CCP's self-correction process. Xi Jinping said in Seattle, USA in 2015 that China will continue to fight corruption like forging iron. We need hard tools to forge iron, and the forger is CCP. All sensible Chinese people should realize that only under the leadership of CCP who has come onto the battlefield with a light pack, clear purpose and strong will can we really "get strong".

IV

Since Marxism was passed into China, Chinese nation went onto the journey of great rejuvenation and walked into a bright future under the leadership of CCP. Marxism became a strong thought weapon guiding rejuvenation of Chinese nation. The CCP armed with Marxism became the backbone of Chinese nations' rejuvenation process. To adhere to, strengthen and improve CCP's leadership in the process of "getting strong", we must adhere to the guidance of Marxist political party theory. Marxist political party theory is inseparable from Marxist people's principal position theory. As a Marxist political party, CCP is fully dedicated to the people. Providing happiness for the people and leading Chinese nation to rejuvenation is CCP's initial intention and mission. National rejuvenation is the people's cause and the joint cause of Chinese nation. Fulfillment of this mission requires active participation and hard work of the people. We will form a grand momentum only if we can gather people's heart, strength and intelligence. And only all-conquering willpower can lead us forward with overwhelming momentum on the journey of national rejuvenation. Mr. Mao Zedong pointed out that only people are the force creating world history. The great cause of "getting strong" is inseparable from the guidance of Marxist people's principal position theory and historical viewpoint of the people. In the past, CCP adhered to the aim of serving the people wholeheartedly, and built an intimate relationship with the people. This was how it made great success in history. In the new journey of "getting strong", we still need the people's support and participation, therefore we should still adhere to the guidance of Marxist people's principal position theory. A Marxist political party can win the support and love of the people and fulfill all causes only when it sincerely trusts, relies on and serves the people.

In western theory, the modern times often refers to the times when subjectivity was liberated. Post-modernism often criticizes modernity in the sense of criticizing subjectivity, believing that modern wars and massacres are social and historical results caused by excessive display of subjectivity. Then, what does subjectivity mean? On one hand, when a modern person is considered a subjective part, he becomes the purpose of his existence and source of life's value. He no longer lives for others or God, but for himself. On the other hand, since the human's existence becomes the source of life's value and meaning, the human will become means to fulfill and satisfy himself. Both individuals and humanity can expand and fulfill themselves only through their own actions, therefore humans become power of existence and driving force of life and social and historical development. In this sense, modernity liberation means to establish the principle of subjectivity that "man owns his life". People's rights, interests, desires and rationality are acknowledged, and they can fulfill themselves with rights of freedom, equality and democracy. In other words, people are considered as individuals liberated from various autocratic systems and abstinence. Modern subjectivity mainly refers to subjectivity in the above sense. Abstract citizen in modern political philosophy and "economic man" in national economy have typically embodied the concept of modern subjectivity, with its core at the principle of individualism and self-centeredness. Marx pointed out that individualism and egoism are the basic principles of modern civil society.

Marxism has confirmed the huge historical significance of modern individual liberation and acknowledged that establishment of modern subjectivity is a great historical advancement, and that history is but activities of people seeking their own purpose. But at the theoretical basis of historical materialism, Marxism does not emphasize the subjectivity of independent individual awareness, but the people's principal position. Subjectivity theory of Marxism is people's principal position theory. Marx pointed out with criticism that individual subjectivity is the product of modern social history and only the conceptual abstraction of common living conditions in capitalism. The theory of natural rights and "economic man" consider historical products as "absolute" without history. Marxism believes that such a concept of modern subjectivity is a form of abstract humanism. In the view of historical materialism, such abstract humanism starts from abstract humans instead of humans in reality. Marx and Engels have stipulated the starting point of historical materialism as "humans in reality". Humans in reality was explained in *The German Ideology* co-authored by them. Humans in reality means humans who are carrying out production and re-production of living materials, whose needs are constantly changing during production, and who produce life of their own and others. The production and re-production of life is the unity of natural and social processes. Historical materialism believes that we should comprehend social history by starting from living, production and re-production of humans in reality, or the practice of production; and should not comprehend historical movement by starting from ideological concepts. Social existence is the process of production and re-production of social life. The evolution of social history is not actualized by subjective consciousness or individual spirit, but a process of objective social production development.

This is the basic thought of historical materialism in words "social existence determines social consciousness" or "economic basis determines superstructure". The above thought brought about fundamental change of social historical view. While explaining materialist conception of history, Lenin pointed out: "The discovery of, or more exactly, the promotion and application of materialism in social phenomenon field has eliminated two major shortcomings of previous historical theories. Firstly, previous historical theories only studied people's motivation in historical activities, but did not study the cause of such motivation, explore the objective regularity of social relation development, or consider the extent of material production development as source of these relations. Secondly, previous historical theories neglected the residential masses' activities, and only historical materialism enables us, for the first time to study people's social conditions of living and variations of these conditions with the precision of natural science." Because Marxism studies social history in the aspect of people's life and social conditions, it does not remain on defense of individual abstract rights or construe the significance of modern liberation in the sense of subjectivity liberation. According to the view of historical materialism, people's production and life created history. The people not only created material and spiritual wealth, but push forward historical development in critical times of history. Adhering to people's principal position means to analyze the people's actual living situation and how they push forward social historical development. Based on this thought, Marxism adheres to people's central position, dedication for the people, reliance on the people, defense of people's political rights, satisfaction of people's material interests, and arouse of people's enthusiasm. Marxist political parties are those who adhere to people's principal position theory, consider people's cause as its own cause, and do not have any special interest other than people's interests. While leading Chinese people to "get strong", CCP must adhere to Marxist guidance in terms of people's principal position theory.

Marxist people's principal position theory is different from the people-oriented thought in the old days. People-oriented thought serves, in fact, the feudal officials. The rulers care for the people and follow people's will in order for their regime to last through generations. In the people-oriented thought, people do not have an equal position or equal rights in the sense of legal rights, not to mention being considered creators of history or fundamental purpose of value. Certainly, people's principal position theory in historical materialism is also different from modern abstract humanism or modern democracy. People's principal position theory does not construe subjectivity in the sense of acquiring abstract rights. It emphasizes not liberation from autocracy or hierarchy and establishment of the individual's principal position, but explains people's principal position and realization of people's interests from the angles of social and historical relations in reality and historical movements, and provides a richer and profounder historical connotation for people's principal position. In this sense, we believe historical materialism is the real theory of democracy, and the social historical theory which, for the first time, starts from the people. For the first time, it has demonstrated people's principal position on the level of historical views. It has denied the historical viewpoint of heroes in which heroes create history, and the historical fatalism which emphasizes self-development of history, and it has truly found the basic power and movement mechanism of historical development. Here, the conflicts between voluntarism and mechanical determinism, subjectivity and objectivity, leaders and the people have been eliminated. More importantly, such a materialist historical view does not comprehend liberation of subjectivity from the angle of abstract rights, but comprehend the extent of liberation based on people's actual material living standards. It encourages satisfaction of people's requirements and change of social reality. After liberation of modern abstract rights, a new liberation theory appeared, and acquisition of abstract political rights is no longer considered the fundamental characteristic of subjectivity liberation. On the basis of criticizing modern liberation of subjectivity, Marxist people's principal position theory put forward the path of liberation for entire humanity, enriched the connotation of subjectivity liberation and provided a profound theoretical basis for political practice in reality.

In the Party's 19th NC report, President Xi Jinping pointed out: "People are creators of history and basic force determining the future and destiny of the Party and country. We must adhere to people's principal position, serve public interests, govern the country for the people, devote ourselves to serving the people, place people at the center of all governance activities, strive for people's happiness, and make historical achievements by relying on people." People's principal position theory is the basic standpoint of Marxism and includes connotations on multiple sides and levels. Next, we'll explain the importance of people's principal position theory by discussing the people as the subject of rights, interests and practice. Without extensive participation of the people, tremendous power cannot be generated, and China cannot get strong. If we cannot defend people's rights and satisfy people's interests, only the strong will benefit if we, somehow, get strong, and since we have deviated from our initial intention, we cannot win the love and support of the people, and our prosperity cannot last. Only when we adhere to people's principal position theory and implement this theory in practice on all sides can China really get strong, and such a strong country can represent people's will and defend people's interests.

To adhere to Marxist people's principal position theory, we should first assure and protect people's democratic rights, and develop and improve socialist democracy. Democracy is the precondition of socialism, and in both theory and practice, democracy is required in socialism. Certainly, democracy has many forms, and it does not equal to socialism. In this regard, there are often some vague or even wrong understandings which confuse theory and bring disasters in practice. To adhere to Marxist people's principal position theory, we must assure that people are the subject of rights, and all power of the country is rooted in the people. To fulfill the mission of "getting strong", we must protect people's political rights and arouse their enthusiasm. Only in this way can we gather the strength required to rejuvenate Chinese nation.

Some people consider freedom and democracy as monopoly of capitalism, and believe that only universal suffrage, multi-party system and separation of powers are called democracy. Modern modes of freedom and democracy are considered as the unique criteria, and only their approximation is called freedom and democracy. In this viewpoint, Marxism and socialism became the contrary to freedom and democracy. Among people holding this viewpoint, some criticize Marxism, but strangely, some adhere to Marxism. In their understanding, freedom and democracy are derogatory terms in Marxist language, as if Marxism is the enemy of freedom and democracy, we don't discuss freedom and democracy in Marxism, and freedom and democracy is the monopoly of capitalist civilization. Under the pressure of discourse on freedom and democracy, socialist countries can only passively defend itself. With weakening of power of discourse, they dare not raise the flag of freedom and democracy with courage. Our country's *Constitution* has clearly stipulated its nature as people's democratic dictatorship, and assigned basic democratic rights and obligations to citizens. In the Party's 19th NC report, Xi Jinping pointed out: "We are a socialist country of people's democratic dictatorship led by the workers' class and based on worker-peasant alliance. All power of the country belongs to the people. Our socialist democracy is the broadest, most genuine and most effective democracy protecting people's basic interests. Developing socialist democratic politics means to reflect people's will, protect people's rights and interests, arouse people's creativity, and ensure people's principal position with the country's system." The main point of Marxist people's principal position theory is that people, as citizens, are the subject of rights. The citizens' democratic rights are defended and protected. Only when people's democratic rights are fully protected can we invite people's active participation and truly serve the people. We should properly understand Marxist democratic theory and its dialectical standing on modern democracy, stand against all thought trends denying socialist democracy, and guide the construction of socialist democracy with Marxist theory in order to create a lively political situation and lay a solid political foundation for Chinese nation to "get strong".

Marxism has critically inherited modern democracy. It affirms protection of people's democratic rights, but it also believes we cannot stay on the level of abstract rights. According to Marx' viewpoint, capitalist democracy standing against feudal hierarchy and autocracy is the fruit of modern liberation and has affirmed people's democratic rights. Modern democracy has overthrown the power structure based on secular and theocratic hierarchy, considers freedom and equality as basic principles of public life, acknowledges people's rights equally, and considers citizens as equal individuals regardless of blood, region, religion, economy and knowledge. This is the essence of modern democracy. Marx praised "self-awareness" in his doctor's thesis. In fact, he was calling for modern people's awakening, defending enlightenment's subjectivity and requesting equality and freedom. In the political comment of *Rhine*, he called for freedom of speech and publication and criticized religious and secular autocracy. He was actually calling for freedom and democracy. Or in other words, the call for modern freedom and democracy is the starting point of Marxism, and Marx has been working for people's freedom and democracy all his life. However, by criticizing modern freedom and democracy as well as capitalist production mode and their relation, Marx passed on the message that modern liberation is only political liberation in form and abstraction. Citizens acquired abstract rights of freedom and democracy, but actually live in bondage, slavery and inequality. Therefore, democracy of modern capitalism is only formal and abstract democracy. Just as modern Marxist Ellen Wood pointed out, real democracy essentially stands against capitalism. Only socialism or communist can protect people's democratic rights and surpass modern capitalist democracy which only realizes abstract rights.

It can be clearly pointed out that defending people's rights and principal position is the basic requirement of Marxist people's principal position theory. Without freedom and democracy, socialism cannot be called "socialism" at all. For a socialist regime, social and economy development is the precondition. Poverty is not socialism, but mere economic development is not socialism, either. Socialism should demonstrate a new mode of living surpassing freedom and democracy of modern capitalism. When the legitimacy foundation of the regime set up by revolution fades out, we cannot build our legitimacy solely on economic development. It is mistaken to consider humans as simple economic creatures as if they only need material and economic satisfaction. And it is way too simple to believe that if we construct good economy, we are rest assured about stability of the regime because Soviet Union collapsed due to economic problems. Today, if we want to "get strong", we must adhere to Marxist people's principal position theory and construct a highly democratic socialist mode of living. We will encounter big problems if we neglect the importance and urgency of , or fail to obey the principles and direction of democracy construction. While carrying out construction under

Marxism's guidance, we must adopt socialist democracy in our thinking and implement such thought in action.

In socialist democratic construction, we must adhere to the guidance of Marxist theory and make clear the distinction and connection between Marxist concept of freedom and democracy and modern theory of freedom and democracy. The key to this question is to reveal the profound difference between socialist democracy and capitalist democracy, highlight the essential requirements of socialist democracy, construct a political civilization based on the above requirements, and emphasize the uniqueness and advancement of democratic construction. We should not easily cede our territory of freedom and democracy and regard the formal freedom and democracy of modern capitalism as the sole standard. The distinction has been made clear by classic authors of Marxism. We are not discussing whether we need democracy in socialism, but what kind of democracy is required, and in what way we shall guarantee people's democratic rights.

While following Marxist guidance in socialist construction, we should also make clear the difference between socialist democracy and democratic socialism. As a social trend, democratic socialism has a complex connection with Marxism. Democratic socialism proposes to join the regime through parliament election, improve workers' living condition, influence the direction of capitalist development, and finally enter the stage of socialism in a peaceful way. In the choice between revolution and reform, democratic socialism proposes to reform capitalism, and realize socialism in a democratic way under capitalist conditions. Because of change of social and historical conditions, many political schools and theoretical schools holding the view of democratic socialism basically abandoned the path of socialism. Because real socialism was mistakenly criticized by some as revolutionary, autocratic and violent, democratic socialism became the tool used to criticize real socialism and place the practice of scientific socialism in contrast to democracy and freedom. Democracy discussed in democratic socialism is formal, competitive and abstract, and is far behind the level of freedom and democracy discussed in Marxism; while socialist democracy is about how socialism is constituted, and how a socialist society constructs and promotes people's democracy. If democratic socialism carries reforming significance in capitalist countries, promoting such socialism in socialist countries is actually a backward step neglecting socialist principles.

During construction and practice of socialist democracy, we should handle the relationship between ideal freedom and democracy and restrictions in real world in a dialectical way. Only with Marxist guidance can we develop freedom and democracy as part of people's democracy, establish our standing on the side of the people, and ensure proper direction of democratic construction. Meanwhile, we must realize that we have special historical backgrounds and realistic conditions in socialist construction, we will stay in the beginning stage of socialism for a long time, and the real and complete democracy depicted in Marxist classic authors have not been realized. But it is our firm goal, and we don't leave it to the future; instead, we gradually realize this goal in every step of practice. In this way, theory and practice will form a benign interactive relation, persuasive force and orientation. In this sense, the direction of socialist democracy carries great significance.

Today, we are demonstrating a distinctive and strong expectation for construction of freedom and democracy. The distinction mainly refers to principles instead of details. Our expectation has arrived at the extent of urgency as well as pressure on political system reform. Collapse of Soviet Union has clearly indicated that it is wrong to neglect socialist democracy or have a wrong direction of democratic and political construction. In all cases, we should raise the flag of, and promote socialist democracy. "The Party's leadership, people's principal position and governance according to law are the necessary requirements of socialist political development. We must adhere to the pathway of socialism with Chinese characteristics, follow and improve the system of people's congress, multi-party cooperation and political consultation led by CCP, regional ethnic autonomy and grass-root people's autonomy, strengthen and develop the widest patriotic united front, develop socialist consultative democracy, improve democratic system, enrich democratic forms, expand democratic channels, and make sure people's principal position is implemented in political and social life of the country." By continuous exploration in construction practice, we have made progress on the pathway of socialism with Chinese characteristics, and people's democracy and freedom are protected by our system and law. The key is to promote democracy and cultivate democratic spirit in reality, and transform democracy into a habit and mode of life. By walking on this pathway and conducting exploration, we will certain create a new situation of free and democratic living, and change the appearance of socialism which is currently separated from freedom and democracy.

According to people's principal position theory, people are the subject of rights, all power of the nation belongs to the people, and people have basic civilian rights and bear the corresponding civilian obligations. People are creators of history, and all work of Marxist political party is centered on the people. The Marxist political party has no special interest of its own, but is dedicated to the people's interests. Increasing people's happiness is the basic purpose of the Marxist political party. The Party's 19th NC pointed out we should ensure and improve people's livelihood during development and place people at the center. "Improving people's livelihood and happiness is the basic purpose of development. We must serve people's interests, help them solve difficulties, improve their livelihood during development, facilitate social fairness and justice, and provide nurturing for the young, education for the students, gains for the laboring, medicine for the sick, care for the elderly, residence for the homeless and support for the weakness. We should conduct poverty alleviation, ensure all people can benefit from our development, and keep promoting comprehensive development of humans and common prosperity. While constructing a peaceful country, we will strengthen and innovate social governance, maintain harmony and stability of society, ensure lasting political stability and facilitate peaceful living and working." Based on the basic principles of Marxism and historical materialism, Mao Zedong stipulated wholehearted service for the people as the basic purpose of CCP. To lead Chinese people to "get strong", we must adhere to people's principal position theory as our basic principle, always remind ourselves of our initial intention, and share the same fate with the people.

"Serving people wholeheartedly" has embodied the people's principal position theory of historical materialism, and is the brief and vivid summary of people's principal position theory in Marxism. This purpose has revealed the distinction between people's principal position theory of Marxism and modern individual subjectivity. Marxist people's principal position theory does not, in an abstract sense, emphasize people's rights, struggling for people's freedom, equality and democracy, liberation of the people from hierarchy system and autocracy and their transformation into independent individuals in modern legal rights. The purpose of Marxism is humanity's comprehensive liberation. Marxists not only fight for people's democratic rights, but try their best to provide people with realistic necessities and happiness on all sides. The fundamental purpose is to realize people's interests. In Marxist theory, people are not only owners of rights or citizens in political life, but creators and driving force of history; therefore they deserve to enjoy the fruit of historical development. Marxist political parties should represent, pursue and realize people's interests. Mr. Mao Zedong has grasped the core of people's principal position theory in Marxism, and put forward the thought of "serving the people" in his speech commemorating Zhang Side. Mao

Zedong pointed out: "Our Communist Party and the Eight Route Army and New Fourth Army led by Communist Party are revolutionary armies. Our armies are dedicated to liberating people and people's interests." Later, in the article *On Coalition Government*, Mao Zedong pointed out again: "Standing close with Chinese people and serving Chinese people wholeheartedly is the sole purpose of our army." The purpose of "serving people wholeheartedly" put forth by Mao Zedong is the reflection and development of Marxist people's principal position theory in practice, and a sinicized form of the theory. President Xi Jinping pointed out in the forum commemorating the 120th anniversary of Mao Zedong's birth: "Serving people wholeheartedly is the starting point and foothold of all actions of the Party, and the basic sign of distinction between our Party and all other political parties. All work of our Party must be measured against the highest standard, which is the basic interests of the people. The effectiveness of our work is judged by whether the people have gained benefit, the people's life has been improved and people's rights and interests have been protected." Only when we serve the people wholeheartedly can we gain the wide support of the people and lead them to accomplish great rejuvenation of Chinese nation.

Since the CCP has been serving the people wholeheartedly and staying close with the people, it has won the love and support of the people in wars and peaceful periods. Membership of the Party became a brilliant title representing open-minded individuals and activists. It is not only a political identity, but also a symbol of nobility in moral character. Serving the people is the honorable mission of Communists. But in recent years, with the development of socialist market economy and division of social interests, some people acquired power and special interests, and forgot the mission of serving the people. In this scenario, some people even propose that CCP, as a governing party, should become a general social organization like western political parties, and the concept of the people should be replaced by "citizens" in a law-based society. They request to set out boundaries between political organizations and citizens, and between public power and private affairs. They say public power and resources cannot be used to serve private affairs. The purpose of serving people wholeheartedly is met with various challenges under new historical conditions. In essence, the question arose that whether we should still adhere to Marxist people's principal position theory and the initial heart of CCP, and whether CCP still has a legitimate and justified foundation of governance.

When Xi Jinping was in a group study of historical materialism with the Political Bureau of the CPC Central Committee, he emphasized that we should acquire the viewpoint that the people are creators of history, and should stay close with the people to push forward our cause. Realizing, maintaining and developing the fundamental interests of the people is considered the starting point and foothold of all work, and results of development should be shared by all people. Only in this way can we make success in reform. In this regard, the Party's 19th NC report has further explanation: "We can fulfill our mission only if we keep our initial heart. The initial heart and mission of Chinese Communists are to seek happiness for Chinese people and accomplish national rejuvenation. The initial heart and mission is the momentum encouraging Chinese Communist to march forward. All comrades of the party must share the same heart and fate with the people, work for the people's happy life, march forward with a strong willpower, and continue to achieve the purpose of national rejuvenation." This is the latest description of the requirement to adhere to people's principal position theory and serve the people wholeheartedly. In the historical journey of national rejuvenation, we must adhere to people's principal position theory and the purpose of serving the people wholeheartedly in order to fulfill the mission of "getting strong". Only when we have earned the love and support of the people can we gather the people's effort and transform our country into a prosperous, democratic, civilized, harmonious, beautiful, and modernized socialist country.

In early works of Marx and Engels, they said: "History is no other than activities of people who pursue their purpose." This sentence briefly summarized the historical concept of modern subjectivity and emphasized the role of humans in history. Humans are the subject of historical activities. On one hand, humans are the purpose of historical activities, and the existence of humans is the source of value and significance. On the other hand, humans are the power of historical advancement. Through pursuit for their own purpose, humans push forward historical advancement. The above concept of subjectivity denied the historical concept of fatalism and mechanical determinism, and considers history as a realistic process pushed forward by subjective practice instead of dominated by some external mystical power. Certainly, the historical concept of subjectivity in historical materialism also objects to voluntarism and heroism. Historical materialism highlights subjective spirit creating history and that theoretical understanding aims at changing reality. According to the basic principles of historical materialism and Marxist historical viewpoint, the people are subjects creating history, and the people's practice pushes forward historical advancement. Marxist people's principal position theory calls for defense of the people's subjective rights and satisfaction of people's interests, and emphasizes that we should respect the people's pioneering spirit, arouse their passion in creating history, and enable them to push forward advancement of history and humanity. To progress from the stage of "getting rich" to "getting strong", we must further arouse people's subjective spirit, enthusiasm, initiative and creativity, and enable them to participate in the new journey of great rejuvenation. Only in this way can we gather the crowds' wisdom and strength and achieve the purpose of building a socialist, modernized and strong country.

In the times of revolutionary wars, we overcame all difficulties, gained victory of revolution, overthrew the "three big mountains", and founded the People's Republic of China because of the broad participation, active support, sacrifice and devotion of the people. And now, in the times of construction, we achieved success with millions of ordinary individuals working days and nights under CCP's leadership. During construction of socialism with Chinese characteristics, the people created one after another miracles with their pioneering spirit and hard-working attitude, and China made great advancement in society and economy. With only 40 years, we completed the journey which western developed countries too decades or even a hundred years to complete, and quickly realized the goal of "getting rich". Now China has become the second largest economy. Although we are still insufficient and unbalanced in economy, no one will connect China with poverty. We made such a brilliant achievement because we aroused people's creative passion and affirmed their subjectivity spirit. To gather strength and "get strong", we must trust and rely on people, continue to arouse the people's subjective spirit, and guide our practice with Marxist people's principal position theory.

To adhere to people's principal position in Marxism and arouse people's subjective spirit in practice, we need to, in a dialectical view, analyze the relationship between great historical persons, advanced political parties and the people. Marxism is a dialectical materialism. While affirming the people's principal position, it does not deny the historical role of excellent people, and the huge contribution of leaders to historical advancement. And we don't deny the effect of advanced political parties in leading the times and creating history. While discussing the huge historical effect of great persons, Marxist theorist Plekhanov pointed out: "Great persons are indeed initiators, because their learning is more than others and their wish is stronger than others. They point out new social demands arising from social relation development, and assume responsibility for such demands." Great persons are those with far sight who can point out the direction at critical moments and lead people to realize the ideal goal. Affirming people's subjectivity in creating history does not mean denying the importance of great persons appearing in people's practice and guiding people's practice. Meanwhile, historical viewpoint of the people does not deny the contribution of advanced political parties in organization, promotion and facilitation while people are creating history. Because of the leadership and organization of advanced political parties, the people can play an active role in creating history. Therefore, in the new journey of "getting strong", we should adhere to both people's principal position and the Party's leadership, and should not place them at opposite positions. The Party's people path is a precious tool used to handle the relationship between leaders, the political party and the people. President Xi Jinping pointed out: "People path is our lifeline and basic path of work, and a precious tool used to maintain vitality and fighting capacity. No matter in the past, present or future, we should always work for, rely on, and stay close with the people, transform the Party's correct proposal into people's conscious action, and implement the people path in all activities of national governance."

In this regard, some people in the circle of domestic theory and social opinions purposely created conflicts between "elitism" and "populism". From an abstract standpoint, they place ordinary people in opposition to social elites, and even try to create conflicts and social disruption between the two. Some people hold an abstract people's standpoint, as if only they are representing people's interests. They take advantage of some people's emotions and particular events to provoke social conflicts, oppose to social elites, science and rationality, and even deny the Party's leadership. Finally, they slid to an abstract standpoint of populism. Some people, on the contrary, look down upon people from a high standing. They disrespect the people's interests, refuse to serve the people, and belittle the people's role. Since Marxist historical viewpoint of the people adheres to people's principal position theory, service for the people and reliance on the people, we must oppose to such an abstract people's standpoint and abstract elites' standpoint, hear the voice of the people, learn from the people, organize the people's creativity and enthusiasm in social construction, and form a tremendous force to achieve national rejuvenation.

V

By reviewing history, we know Mao Zedong's words of pride on the eve of new China's founding: "Since Chinese people learned Marxism-Leninism, they turned from passive to active in spirit. The times in world history when Chinese people and culture are looked down upon ended at that point." On the basic of "standing up" and "getting rich", when China went further to "get strong", our activity in spirit and culture should be demonstrated in a more outstanding and comprehensive manner. After the 18th NC of the Party, the Central Party Committee centered on Xi Jinping gradually put forward and explained, on the basis of "three confidences" the concept of "cultural confidence", and believe that culture confidence is "confidence more basic, wider and profounder". It can be said that our purpose to "get strong" is calling for self-improvement and self-confidence in spiritual culture.

As far as spiritual culture is concerned, many schools of thought in philosophy and social sciences made excellent explanations, but the culture based on "socialism with Chinese characteristics" will certainly need Marxist guidance. Marxism has crossed over the idealist error zone and scientifically set out the role of humans' spiritual factors in social life and practice; and especially, it put forward the concept of "ideology" which is a spiritual factor defining people's social and class characteristics. The Party's 19th NC report emphasized: "Socialist culture with Chinese characteristics is a strong spiritual force motivating people of all ethnic to make advancement." It has displayed the pillar role of spiritual culture and reflected confirmation and extension of sinicized Marxism in the times as well as the modern value of Marxist ideological theory.

The materialist historical viewpoint of Marxism has scientifically analyzed the dialectical movement of "economic basis - superstructure" in human society. On one hand, Marxism considers the mode of production and interaction in people's material life as the basis determining people's all aspects of life, including spiritual life. On the other hand, Marxism believes that the superstructure, including political and legal system and people's "ideology", or viewpoints in law, politics, religion, art and philosophy are reflecting the economic basis. In late years, Engels emphasized to Marxist learners that they should understand materialist conception of history in a comprehensive and dialectical way, and these factors of ideology "have an influence on the process of historical struggle and, in many cases, determine the form of struggle."

It is consistent with Marxist world view to acknowledge ideology's unique role and important influence in historical movement. In materialist dialectical method of Marxism, we do not, as in western philosophy or modern philosophy, make a mechanical dual distinction between matter and spirit, and emotion and rationality, or resort to ridiculous unity such as pineal body or God. Marx has based the unity in humans' emotional practice and believe that humans have a "rich, full and profound feeling". Rational thinking, expectations and designs exist within humans' emotions. In other words, they are an internal link in humans' practice.

The mainstream viewpoint of western philosophy in the past regarded "rationality" as the essential distinction between humans and animals, but Marx abandoned such a partial view of idealism. He advocated material practice. Such practice is general and comprehensive, and not a pure physiological function in flesh. Marx praised in *Das Kapital* that even the worst architect is smarter than a bee, and that affirmed the significance of people's concept in practice. In the classic description of materialist conception of history in Critique of Political Economy, Marx used "ideology", "spiritual life" and "social ideology" in the same category and on the same level. Ideology is also an organic part of people's life and social ability. It can be said that in Marxism's definition of humans, conceptual factors are integrated in the humans' general practice, and therefore also integrated in humans' realistic nature.

Further, as a revolutionary, practical and communist materialism, Marxism emphasizes the leading role of ideological reform in general social reform while explaining the important reforms in social historical movement, especially the critical turning points and moments. Marxism believes that once a theory is understood by the people, it will turn into material strength; and moreover, the communist cause of modern proletarian class quite relies upon such understanding and change. The reason is that a new society of communism cannot nurture itself in an old economic basis. We cannot passively wait until capitalist society to collapse and new society to take shape. Therefore, communist must be consciously created and operated by revolutionary ideology and pioneering teams in the superstructure so that a great social revolution can take place. In this regard, Lenin made a conclusion with brief words: Revolutionary movement cannot take place without a revolutionary theory.

In the great historical practice of "standing up" and "getting rich", Chinese people vividly demonstrated how the theoretical weapon of Marxism guided their practice. Since the October Revolution brought Marxism-Leninism into China, Chinese people exploring the cause of self-rescue made the right choice of the pathway to walk. Especially, Chinese Communists made a theoretical leap of Marxism's

Sinicization and guided the people to found a new China through new democratic revolution. Chinese people stood up since then. The start of new historical cause called "opening and reform" was also attributed to the leading role of ideology. Following the preparatory step of great discussion of truth standards, the Party's Third Plenary Session of the 11th Central Committee brought order out of chaos, and then pushed forward the leap of Marxism's Sinicization and lead Chinese people onto the pathway of socialism with Chinese characteristics. It can be said that Chinese people's liberation of productive force in the process of "getting rich" is inseparable from the thought liberation in "practice is the sole criterion for testing truth" in the beginning. The "second revolution" of reform is inseparable from the "second leap" of Marxism's Sinicization.

Today, on the basis of "standing up" and "getting rich", Chinese people are standing on the new historical journey of "getting strong". We still should pay attention to issues and tasks in the ideological field and adhere to the guiding position of Marxism as our spiritual pillar. Firstly, the pillar effect is represented as a security guarantee and guarding at the bottom line. On the journey of "getting strong", we are faced with difficulties and complex situations; especially, the questioning and challenge in the ideological field are more than those in the process of "standing up" and "getting rich", and we may easily make destructive mistakes if we are careless. Therefore, the Central Party Committee centered on Mr. Xi Jinping repeatedly emphasized the importance of ideological safety. He emphasized that Marxism is our "special skill" guarding our home. Only if we guard our "home" can we move forward along the right direction and avoid the fate of Soviet Union, which disarmed itself in thought and collapsed. Secondly, the pillar effect is represented as pioneering spirit. At the starting stage of our socialist construction, Mao Zedong mentioned: "A man should have some kind of spirit" in order to motivate the Party and people to overcome difficulties on the way, and he stipulated hardworking and diligence as economic principles. These were not only measures taken, and concepts adopted in material scarcity, but contained productive elements and a way out of poverty. Today, although we made great achievements in national rejuvenation, we still need long-term development to realize the goal of "getting strong", and the process of development needs planning and leadership. President Xi Jinping said: "In terms of development, the concept leads to actions, and is a general element governing the root, direction and long-term progress." When we correct our concept, we are providing driving force for development.

Since ideology reflects the economic basis of society at the root, our ideological work during the process of "getting strong" should be based on our national situation and social system. We should confront and handle all tasks and challenges arising from this basis, and carry out systematic construction in economic and social development and ideological safety. In the stage of "standing up", we launched a great social revolution on the semi-feudal and semi-colonial economic basis, overthrew the "three big mountains" pressuring on Chinese people since the modern times, eradicated spiritual poisoning and destruction left by the old society, and then set up the basis system and material foundation of socialism. We tried our best to cultivate new spiritual culture of socialism. And in the stage of "getting rich", we should adhere to "development is the absolute principle", and "development is the top priority of national governance", gather all strength to construct economy, improve people's material living standards, create the consensus of national rejuvenation on the basis of development, and facilitate the development and prosperity of socialist culture.

Along with opening and reform as well as establishment of socialist market economy, ideology of Chinese society will certainly change, and our ideological work is faced with new challenges. "Old revolution" encountered "new problems", which were not automatically solved while we were "getting rich". The problem was left to the new generation in "getting strong". In the new times, we should carry out ideological work more effectively and right to the point, and create an ideological system with innovation. According to Marxism, economic basis and superstructure are not identical; but united in a dialectical way. Dialectical unity, in this regard, is a movement process from differentiation in identity to selective unity in contradiction. To "get strong", we should complete selection and reconciliation on a higher level.

As we can see, in Marx' direct vision, market is profoundly connected with the social form of modern capitalism. Even if our socialist market economy has taken out the appropriate core of market and enabled it to play an active role, it still carries the original properties with more affinity to capitalist principles; therefore, the ideology arising internally in the market and partially displaying capitalist principles has the soil to grow in China. According to Marx, the market "is the basis and surviving condition of capitalist mode of production", and oppositely, it is "the necessity in capitalism to produce in larger and larger scale to expand world market." The start point of market is an entity of personal interest in which obtaining interests is the driving force of economic activity. Such an entity and force is able to cycle and expand, and stimulate personal enthusiasm in person to person competition. Market competition creates efficiency, drives growth of productive force and increases social wealth.

But in western capitalist world, capital makes full use of, without limit, the internal mechanism of market. It indulges people and encourages them to pursue the biggest interest, and as a result, it created and strengthened ideologies including consumerism, hedonism and individualism suitable for capitalist economic basis. Socialist countries adopt market economy because market plays an active role in driving interest and efficiency, and objectively, the social productive force. If we are making use of the efficiency factor of market economy under socialist conditions, we must carefully consider the negative sides of market as well as its ideological by-products.

The superiority of socialist market economy depends on its system arrangements and ideological shaping which makes market better than capitalism in fulfilling people's wish. Capitalist countries adopt market economy because they wish to increase the interests and efficiency of capital, and finally expand capital so that the wealth efficiently generated by the market is not mainly owned by laborers. Besides, capital expansion includes re-definition and denial of wealth. The celebrated western economist Commons described the market system of capitalism: In the market, "Goods are exchanged not in the sense of 'delivery', but the assignment and acquisition of future ownership of material objects between individuals", and is "the transfer of ownership". The "value" and "expansion" pursued by capitalism is accumulation of abstract ownership symbols, which, over time, are gradually manifest as abstract and virtual growth from goods to value and from real industry to finance and virtual economy.

Socialism with Chinese characteristics is fundamentally different from the above system. We are realizing socialist purpose by using market according to the basic principles of Marxism. Such use indicates, firstly, our respect for, and our respond to the people's request for economic benefits. Social members are encouraged to labor and operate their business legitimately and honestly, and market resources are so allocated that material productive force is liberated and developed. The enthusiasm of individuals, society and country is aroused to increase the quantity of social wealth and improve people's livelihood. Therefore, the socialist nature requires the people to form a community of interest, and in terms of ideology, it requires the people to make use of subjective spirit, and work hard together for a common dream. In the stage of "getting rich", Deng Xiaoping pointed out that we should pay attention to the issue of allocation when we are economically better. In the new times of "getting strong", we should deepen our reform, place people at the center of development, and share benefits of development with the people. Only in this way can we guarantee the socialist direction of modernization construction and market economy, and that the Chinese dream is people's dream at the end.

Our guiding ideal should contain ambitious goals and be realistic. While keeping our initial heart, we should create new knowledge and plans. Xi Jinping said we should keep our noble dream of communism in the heart, follow the basic guideline and principles of the Party in the beginning stage of socialism, and perform every task carefully. Today, when China is "getting strong" with increased comprehensive strength, cultural influence, global influence and exemplary effect, we should further push forward the development of Marxism under Marxist guidance, make new explanations in the new times, contribute Chinese wisdom to the world, and win spiritual initiative again. In other words, the process China "gets strong" is also the process Marxism walks from down time to rejuvenation. Marxism and the increased strength of China will influence and facilitate each other. China's Marxism in the 21st century will become a great form of Marxism in history.

Besides internal strength of economic basis and ideology, China is facing more direct opponents in ideology in the process of "getting strong". The first is the attack and "westernization" seduction from western capitalist countries. And there is the thought trend of "westernization" in China which blindly adores western countries. The western capitalist world holds enmity against socialism, but Chinese Communist have clearly realized, before the founding of new China, that their attacks will take the form of "sugar candies" over time. And the western world headed by America put up the strategy of "peaceful transformation", trying to find a breakthrough in ideology, and break down socialist countries from the inside by controlling the thoughts of their people and even government officials. When China has opened up, reformed and went onto the pathway of socialism with Chinese characteristics, the western world seems to have found an "opportunity" and intensified their effort in threat, penetration, and overthrowing. Since the 21ˢᵗ century, we are integrated into the trend of economic globalization and increased our participation in international politics. At this time, the western world's ideological attacks such as "color revolution" and "universal value" are increasing in intensity.

The elementary version of "westernization" thought trend is "full westernization", or "western-centeredness", which means adoration of national strength and high living standard of western countries. Such an ideology directly reflects western advantages and their offensive position since the modern times. With a strong national strength, western countries launched invasions on all sides including military, politics, economy and thought. Consequently, the people of weak countries unconsciously accepted the western modernization picture, and China had the same experience as an ancient civilization. In the particular historical movement, the "west" and "east", as names of geographical location, were provided with heavy social connotation, as if "west" means "modern", and "east" means "traditional". The "west" became general standard in "world history" and stipulated the development direction of other parts of the world. The elements and characteristics of western Europe arising since late medieval times and matured afterwards, such as urban industry and commerce, big machine industry, world market, citizen society, national country, science and technology, and rational morality, art and religion have been given the "western" label, and spread across the world with the expansion of western civilization.

The modern history of other parts of the world, including China has historical relations with their tradition. Although they have, more or less, suspects and reflections on the "west", but in general, they cannot go against the trend of "westernization", and such "westernization" is deeply imprinted in China's modern memory, and most of it has lasted till today. Just as Mao Zedong said: "The only way to rescue the country is to reform, and the only way to reform is to learn from foreign countries. At that time, only western capitalist countries were advanced, because they successfully built up capitalist modern countries. The Japanese did great by learning from the west, so Chinese people also wanted to learn from the

Japanese." But historical lessons taught us that full westernization or the path of the west was not practicable, so we broke through the thought pattern of "westernization".

Secondly, Chinese people gradually accepted Marxism and found a positive direction. The CCP led Chinese people to launch a great social revolution and "stand up" by founding the new China, and "got rich" by liberating and developing productive force. We broke through "full westernization" and "western-centeredness" by walking our own path, a non-western path. On this basis, in order to "get strong", we need to advance along the path we built up, and further increase our self-confidence, create a theoretical story of China with Marxist standpoint, viewpoint and methods, put up a Chinese version of modernization, and refute "full westernization" and "western-centeredness". Objectively, most of the above elements of modernization are the necessary trend of historical development, but we cannot tie them up with "west" and deny other possible or better pathways of building a prosperous civilization. To "get strong", we should break though the conventional thinking of many developing and developed countries in both theory and practice, prove that modernization is not equal to westernization and dependency on the west, and provide a model and choice to be learned from for human civilization.

An "advanced" version of "westernization" trend is to consider human development as equivalent to individualism and rights of freedom in the field of survival mode and social systems, and promote democracy and rule of law in capitalism. Indeed, there were some drawbacks in the past practice of socialist movement. For example, people's living standard was not improved, individual interests were neglected and rejected, and freedom of personality was suppressed. While exploring socialist pathway and finally building up the path of socialism with Chinese characteristics, our country included both problems in its consideration. But in the process of "standing up" and "getting rich", our emphasis was in the former, and we tried to make it clear in theory and improve it in practice because of staged focus of historical task. We still have insufficiency and space to improve in the latter, and we still lack mature discourse in theory.

Especially, when market factor is growing in China and we are transitioning to the market economy system, people have formed and deepened their pursuit for rights and freedom besides material interests. The market itself requires equality and freedom of rights (in form) between individuals, and the creation of a right relation system and guarantee. In Marxist viewpoint, individual rights are economic rights in the first place, and require an economic order based on them, and the capitalist market economy is a trade system based on individual ownership, "a right relation with contract form (whether or not such contracts are enforced by law)" and "a relation of will reflecting economic relations". Correspondingly, political order is the political expression of market economy order on the level of country or law. Therefore, from the historical perspective of individual right changes, the so-called reform and opening-up also inherently involve the redefinition of the social right structure system. Redefinition of the right structure system requires reconfiguration of the relationship between individuals and society, freedom and responsibility, and rights and obligations, adjustment of economic order, political order and ethical order in order to adapt to the modernized market, society and national order. However, at this level, as some western scholars have pointed out, "Civil rights belong to the 18th century, political rights belong to the 19th century, and social rights belong to the 20th century." The west has already completed three stages or three levels of progress and development. Western capitalism has established a first-mover advantage over socialism in the rights system and discourse. Therefore, China's "getting strong" is also responsible for catching up in related fields. As the largest socialist country in the world today, China clearly defines the content of the Chinese plan as a better social system pursued by humanity. We raised the banner of socialism, and with the confidence and posture of "four self-confidences", proclaimed that history is not over, nor can it be terminated. The Chinese road realized the creative combination of the market and socialism, which in turn shaped the formal and free individuals who meet the requirements of the market, promoted the rapid development of citizens' civil rights such as property rights, personal freedom, and freedom of employment. Political rights such as the right to know, the right to express, the right to vote, the right to monitor, and the right to participate have been guaranteed. China accelerated social construction and governance, actively cultivated a rich social soil for the generation and growth of citizens' individual rights, released the vitality and creativity of all aspects of society, opened up the historical process of China's system reform and system construction in all aspects, and actively built a modern market, political society, and civil society that adapt to the basic socialist institutional framework. The above are the unique expression and realistic expansion of the logic of individual rights that was first born in the modern western civilization in the path of reform and development in contemporary China.

China is gradually "getting strong" and making progress in national rejuvenation. Our cultural self-confidence is increasing and "westernization" trend is declining. In this situation, we should pay attention to a different trend; i.e. prevent blind arrogance about China's "tradition" and a tendency of cultural conservatism. Scientific positioning of "China" is the manifestation of "ancient-present-east-west" problem in the new times, and an important subject during construction of socialist culture with Chinese characteristics. Due to our inappropriate conclusions on past experience of exploration and the development model of certain countries and districts in eastern Asia, our insufficient reflections on the negative sides of western capitalist development, and partial use and understanding of the success experience and theories of Chinese path, the thought trend of locality based on "Chinese tradition" went up in recent years. Some people picked up the theory pattern of "ancient civilization restoration" and "ancient Chinese studies as the basis", considered traditional Chinese culture as the basis, and advocated to degrade western tradition as the "end" or "use", They also belittle Marxism, which is the basis of our country, as the "western thought".

The key to dispute is to consider the relationship between Chinese path and factors such as Chinese culture and tradition. Socialist path with Chinese characteristics is the result of Marxism's Sinicization, and both the Party and the people agree to absorb China's cultural roots and tradition, and develop our Chinese style. However, some viewpoints went past the above reasonable boundary and believe that China's culture and civilization should be highlighted in

Chinese path, and the socialist characteristics should be weakened. Among them, some new Confucian scholars in the trend of cultural conservatism proposed to replace Marx with Confucius. Even among those who truly support Marxism and socialism, some propose to integrate traditional Chinese culture more deeply in socialism with Chinese characteristics, connect our guiding thought to tradition, and formulate a "Chinese" civilization plan in which Marxism becomes invisible.

In this regard, we must emphasize that the basis of Chinese path is still Marxism, and we must adhere to the guiding position of Marxism and socialism, and should not replace Marxism and socialism with elements such as traditional culture and civilized country. The Chinese path was built up during modernization and Sinicization of Marxism. The continuation and extension of Chinese path requires us to carry on with Marxism's Sinicization and modernization, and guide our cause by using an evolving version of Marxism. In the theoretical and political language of the Party and country, there are words such as "being practical and realistic", "dialectical thinking", "people's livelihood", "fairness and justice". We can find similar wordings in traditional Chinese culture, but the above thought elements are closer to reality, are part of Marxist worldview and methodology, and a reflection of CCP's thought, theory and purpose. In this aspect, China's cultural tradition is adopted in Chinese path mainly as formal elements such as "style", "style of work", "manners".

In *The Communist Manifesto*, Marx and Engels put forward the well-known thought of "two breakups", on one hand to break up with traditional ownership relation in the economic basis field; on the other to break up with traditional concept in the ideological field. The concept as mentioned here, means thought or cultural form deeply connected with old ownership relation and social, economic and political structure and suitable for the basic fact "some people exploit some others" in the past eras, including "religion, morality, philosophy, politics and law". Marx criticized these traditional concepts as basically "thought of the ruling class". Such criticism of Marx also applies to traditional Chinese culture. Certainly, "total breakup" mentioned in Marxism can be applied only with the dialectical method of criticism and revolution. It is a form of promotion and abandoning, which includes inheritance, assurance and encouragement.

On the Chinese pathway, we inherit and rescue traditional Chinese culture according to criticism principles, and facilitate modern transformation of traditional Chinese culture. Traditional Chinese culture must be transformed based on the times in order to play a positive role, and such transformation must be guided by Marxism. Chinese pathway, as a pathway of modern reform and socialist construction, has inherited and abandoned parts of the tradition of Chinese nation and civilization, and passed on some parts in the context of socialist modernization. While leading our advancement on Chinese pathway, the CCP pushes forward China's modernization, but it is not a pure "industrial party" neglecting socialist principles and Chinese story. It leads people to increase their individual benefits and happiness, but it is not a "livelihood party" neglecting political standing and spiritual belonging. It pursues the Chinese dream of national rejuvenation, but it is not a "Confucian party" detached from China's modernization and socialism. In a group study in the Political Bureau of the CPC Central Committee, Mr. Xi Jinping called Marxism as "special skill guarding our home", and used words such as "original and honest", which clearly pointed out that Marxism is the original principle, and based on Marxism, we learn from and transform the tradition and the west,, develop socialism with Chinese characteristics and enable China to "get strong", including creating new thoughts, culture and tradition of modern China in the cultural field.

After discussing the key points of Marxist ideological theory and the guiding significance of Marxism in our country's ideological field, we should strengthen Marxism's guiding position in the process of "getting strong". To achieve this purpose, we need to adopt several necessary forms and follow several important principles.

Firstly, such guidance must contain the methodology and true spirit of Marxism. Engels once clearly pointed out that Marxist worldview provides not ready-made doctrines, but a starting point and methodology for further research. In this regard, Lukacs pointed out in *History and Class Consciousness* that "original" Marxism does not mean to accept results of Marx' study without criticism or to believe certain arguments or holy books. Instead, "original" in Marxism means methods. In the most general theoretical standing and ordinary methodology, the materialist standpoint, dialectical thinking and practice quality of Marxism have constituted the theoretical basis of scientific socialist cause. Therefore, we should use the fundamental methods in Marxism to analyze problems and perplexities while advancing along the Chinese pathway. By reviewing the history of Marxism's Sinicization, we can discover that China introduced and adhered to Marxist guidance on the level of methodology. China uses Marxism to look upon and deal with actual issues in China, but we cannot say Marxism has provided a ready-made answer. The purpose-driven and realistic attitude enabled Chinese Communists to keep pace with the times and flexibly grasp and use Marxist methods to guide practice in different historical stage and in the face of different social and historical tasks. We need wisdom of the times while "getting strong", therefore we must push forward Marxism's Sinicization and develop scientific socialism of the 21st century under the guidance of Marxism and Marxist scientific methodology.

Secondly, such guidance requires suitable design of the overall system of socialism with Chinese characteristics. While keeping pace with the times, we still need theoretical standing, and cannot change of wisdom of "being practical and realistic" into pragmatic compromise and sophistry. The superstructure of ideology cannot function abstractly when detached from the economic basis. To adapt to the improved socialist market economy system, we should create systems on the Chinese path which are comprehensive, scientific and effective, which include, especially the constitution, legal system and moral codes. In the stages of revolution and construction, CCP demonstrated its leadership and executive force with comprehensive and effective work in thought and organization, but it lagged behind in system construction. When we develop social economy and people are having increased demands for sufficient and balanced development, we need a good and standard system to ensure harmony and coordinated development of society, economy and humans. The past, present and future of Chinese path have regarded the socialist system as basic condition in order to implement socialist principles in a better and more concrete way, and develop and improve ourselves in practice. Only when our system can improve itself will theoretical understanding have a realistic basis, and Marxist ideology will not become a theoretical self-amusement. Under the guidance of the above principle, we should construct a suitable system and create a positive interactive feedback mechanism in which principle guides system and the system guarantees performance of principles.

Thirdly, ideology in a theoretical form should be materialized into ideal faith and internalized into the people's spiritual pursuits. Chinese people always have noble beliefs internalized into continuous spiritual pursuits. For example, Mr. Lu Xun, as we are familiar with, was dedicated to "breaking". He criticized Chinese feudal culture, especially the "cannibalistic" ethical code, the "fake neo-Confucianism", the conservative and retrogressive trend of "promoting national honor in the ancient times"; meanwhile, he was dedicated to "construction" by praising warriors and pioneers. He wrote: "Since the old days, we had hardworking people, tough people, people who plead for others, and people who sacrifice for justice... Even the 'official history' which is almost a genealogy book of emperors cannot cover their brilliance. They are the spine of China." The beliefs and pursuits were continued and promoted in Chinese people's cause of self-rescue in modern times. Mao Zedong commented: "The Chinese nation has the spirit to fight the enemies till the end, the determination to restore past honor based on hard work, and the capacity to stand independently among world nations." The CCP led Chinese people to progress from "standing up", "getting rich" to "getting strong". During this process, we materialized "-ism" of scientific theories into stories of bitterness and struggles, historical necessity into strength fearless of death, and implanted a spiritual spine into the body of scientific theory. In the new times, with sufficient spiritual nurturing, a spiritual outlook of diligence, dream and ambition can be developed during deepened reforms and become an effective mechanism of the CCP to lead modern China on the socialist pathway with Chinese characteristics.

Fourthly, Marxist ideological guidance requires scientific analysis, tolerance and innovation. Marxism is a scientific theory standing at the height of world history, and China should build up its own pathway by learning from both ancient and present and both the east and west, and provide an outlet for modernization and national rejuvenation. Deng Xiaoping pointed out: "To gain the advantages comparable with capitalism, socialist countries must bravely absorb and acquire all results of civilization created by human society." Socialism with Chinese characteristics was formed and developed by mixing Marxism and traditional Chinese and western culture. Just as China needs the leap and breakthrough in Marxism's Sinicization during the process of "standing up" and "getting rich", we must also critically inherit and develop our thoughts under Marxist guidance during the process of "getting strong". Without the most revolutionary dissection, criticism and selective promotion of modern western tradition (especially modern problems and symptoms of capitalism), socialist China would not be able to inherit and promote modern mechanisms such as market, democracy and rule of law. Similarly, without criticism, denial and selective promotion of our tradition, traditional Chinese culture cannot be continued and inherited with vitality in modern China.

VI

Now China is standing on a new historical start point of "getting strong" and welcoming the great leap from "getting rich" to "getting strong". Then, what does "getting strong" mean? And how to "get strong"?

Despite numerous setbacks, China went onto the journey of modernization since the modern times. The process from "standing up" and "getting rich" to "getting strong" is actually the process China advances on the path of modernization, and modernity is realized in China. To study the definition and method of "getting strong", we should know how to face "modernity". In other words, we must observe from a modernity perspective to solve both questions. The fundamental problem of socialist pathway with Chinese characteristics is how to face modernity, which is also the fundamental issue in "getting strong".

Various modernity theories exist in today's world, and Marxist modernity criticism theory has a special position. In the thought field of historical materialism,

Marxism's modernity criticism centered on "capital" reconstructed the basis of modernity criticism and shines its bright light till today. No modernity theory in the world can be compared to Marxist modernity criticism theory, which carries contemporary significance irreplaceable by any modernity theory. Marxist modernity criticism theory contains the theoretical framework and thinking pattern which diagnoses, criticizes and surpasses modernity. Although Marx seldom used the concept of modernity, he profoundly discussed a modernity theory with material content and distinctive characteristics by exploring modern society. When we say studying the process of "getting strong" from the perspective of modernity theory, we are referring to the perspective of Marxist modernity criticism theory. Marxism's realistic significance for modern China and its process of "getting strong" is reflected in Marxist modernity criticism theory's guiding role on our journey of "getting strong".

We are accustomed to name Marx' relevant research of modernity as "modernity criticism theory". It can easily cause a misunderstanding as if Marx only attach importance to modernity criticism. But this is not a fact. Marx' attitude towards modernity is first to praise. He holds a positive attitude towards modernity of Europe and affirms its role in pushing forward human civilization. Marx' praise for modernity is consistent with his praise for modern human civilization. Driven by other motives, some post-modernists regard Marx as someone who also deny and criticize everything about modernity. When talking about Marx' praise for modernity and modern civilization, we are instantly reminded of *The Communist Manifesto*. Indeed, Marx and Engels' *The Communist Manifesto* can be considered a guideline book of Marxist modernity criticism theory. In the beginning of this book, Marx and Engels led us into the understanding of modern society, and by affirming the brilliance of capital modernity, they set up a bright image of modernity. Marx and Engels said: "It forces all nations -- if they don't want to perish -- to adopt the production mode of capitalist class. It forces them to implement their so-called civilization and become capitalists. In one word, it creates a world based on its looks." This world is one in which capital governs everything, or called "modern society" or "modern history". Marx and Engels

152

summarized the process of establishing modernity. It must be pointed out that according to Marx and Engels, the establishment of modernity, which has liberated human society, is a historical necessity. Because the positive effect of modernity is a certainty, Marx believed that despite so much negative effects modernity has demonstrated, backward and developing countries should still initiate a modernization process and develop themselves.

After stating Marx' affirmation of modernity in the first place, it must be emphasized that Marx was affirming modernity in general instead of partial modernity. Marx regarded the history of modern society as a generalization process and believed modernity has general characteristics. "Modern" and "modernity" were morphological concepts according to Marx. "Based on the concept of production mode, Marx determined the position of modernity in historical morphology, and regarded modernity as a general 'world history era'. In a vertical perspective of diachronism, it equals to 'modern history', and in the horizontal perspective of synchronicity, it equals to 'modern society'. It is connected with the general human history and also forms a concrete whole." Capital is the essential category of modernity, and Marx often name modernity with capital. But according to Marx, capital is not simply a narrow economic concept. The internal principles of capital are spread across modern economy, politics, culture and people's psychology. Capital obviously has general characteristics which indicate general characteristics of modernity. Therefore, Marx' modernity theory is a modernity theory in general. It involves not only one particular aspect in politics, economy or culture, but the entire society.

Because Marx believed modernity is a general concept, he expected modernity's implementation in general and all fields of society instead of only one field. The society should implement modernity in all aspects. Marx criticized modernity of capitalist society because such modernity is partial and covers only one field, i.e. the economy. Criticism against one-sided and abnormal development of the modernity of capitalist society is a major perspective of Marx's criticism against capitalist society. If the modernity of the capitalist society is regarded as "unity modernity", that is, modernity is only realized in the economic field, then Marx criticized this "unity modernity". What Marx requires is "multiple modernity", that is, value is given to modernity in terms of economic development, political construction, cultural innovation, social progress, and modern transformation of people.

Since the founding of new China, it has embarked on the road of "getting rich" on the basis of "standing up". Especially after the implementation of reform and opening up, China has embarked on the fast lane of "getting rich". The chief designer of reform and opening up, Deng Xiaoping, said, "Poverty is not socialism," which awakened the entire Chinese people. After 40 years of unremitting efforts, although the current deep-seated contradictions in the global economic development continue to emerge and the international environment is increasingly unstable, the Chinese economy has been steadily growing, and China became the world's second largest economy with a contribution of more than 30% to world economic growth. China has "become rich", which is an undeniable fact. However, comparing with the Marxist modernity criticism theory, it is not difficult to see that this "getting rich" is mainly the realization of modernity in the economic field. The modernity corresponding to "getting rich" is "partial modernity". Of course, under certain historical conditions, China chooses to achieve modernity in the economic field first, which has its historical inevitability. However, today China stands at a new historical starting point and must realize "comprehensive modernity". It is impossible for China to "get strong" without fully realizing modernity. If China's "getting rich" is linked to "partial modernity", then China's "getting strong" should be linked to "comprehensive modernity". In China, "getting strong" is an upgraded version of "getting rich", and correspondingly, "comprehensive modernity" is also an upgraded version of "partial modernity". Where is the "rich" China headed? The Party's 19th NC put forward the development strategy of "two stages". This "two-step" development strategy comprehensively and vividly described how China has moved from "partial modernity" to "comprehensive modernity".

According to the overall requirements of Marxist modernity criticism theory for modernity, China must comprehensively upgrade material civilization, political civilization, spiritual civilization, social civilization, and ecological civilization, realize the modernization of the country's governance system and governance capabilities, and fully build a prosperous, democratic, civilized, harmonious and beautiful socialist power. If "standing up" mainly focuses on the political level of achieving national independence and people's liberation, that is, on creating a political foundation for the realization of modernity in China, "getting rich" mainly focuses on the economic level of liberating productive forces and improving the people's material living standards, i.e. first focusing on the realization of modernity in the economic field; then, "Strengthening" focuses on achieving the goal of "two 100 years" and the dream of great rejuvenation of the Chinese nation, that is, focusing on realization of comprehensive modernity in the ancient land of China. As far as economic development is concerned, according to the requirements of comprehensive modernity, "strengthening" is reflected in the development of a better quality economy, and the devotion to major changes in the economic structure and development momentum so that technological and innovative factors will gradually become the first economic development power. Of course, according to the requirements of comprehensive modernity, we must follow the principles of modernity in other fields outside the economic field in order to "get strong", such as the improvement of democracy and social welfare, the development of cultural undertakings and the increase of cultural self-confidence, and the remarkable achievements in construction of beautiful China. "partial modernity" brings to China only the modernity element of "rich and strong", while "comprehensive modernity" gives China five modern elements including "rich and strong", "democracy", "civilization", "harmony" and "beauty". The development from "partial modernity" to "comprehensive modernity" is the promotion from a "big country" to a "powerful country", in which the fundamental is the improvement from quantity to quality and from hard power to soft power.

Marx holds a dialectical attitude toward modernity, and while affirming the positive effect of modernity, he criticized the negative effect thereof. Marx' dialectical attitude toward modernity stands against the retrospective denial of modernity in conservative romanticism and the complacent affirmation of modernity in liberalism. In dialectical thinking, Marx profoundly revealed the division and contradiction of modernity. In his viewpoint, affirmation of the positive side of modernity and criticism against its negative side are determined by the dialectical characteristics of modernity itself. Modernity is a contradictory entity with basic characteristics such as conflicts, opposition, separation and paradox. He also pointed out that values of modernity including freedom and equality are limited by material conditions of modern society, modern liberation is only abstract liberation in political sense, and the values of modernity have contradictions with the system of modern society. The modern liberation, as political liberation, put people in life of separated dualism. Through political economic criticism, Marx gained insight into the economic basis of modernity contradiction, and considered such basis as the basic framework of modernity. In this way, Marx praised the huge economic and cultural achievements of modern society and also revealed the distorted modernity scenario as well as its internal division and contradiction. Marx emphasized that modern crisis and turmoil arose from division and contradiction of modernity and its paradox. It must be pointed out that Marx criticized modernity based on "modern social economic principles" instead of a "should be" standing of morality.

Capital is the essential category of modernity, and Marx' criticism against modernity's negative effect is also the criticism against capital. As he believed that modernity contains opposition, conflict, separation and paradox, he also believed capital contains the same. "In Marx' view, modernity's contradiction, namely the 'good sides' and 'bad sides' is related to modern capital principles and is a manifestation of modern society's negativity. Such contradiction is not something we can keep or remove. If capital keeps its basic structure in history, then capitalist mode of production will still be the basis of modernity in existence, and modernity's contradiction will still remain as determined by the nature of capital." Marx clearly pointed out: "The simple concept of capital has contained, potentially, the contradictions which will be revealed afterwards." Indeed, contradiction is contained in the concept of capital. Under the rule of capital, we cannot keep the "good sides" of capital and remove the "bad sides". Of course, in our pursuits for modernity, we cannot only adopt the "good sides" and leave off the "bad sides".

The key here is that capital represents a production relation in itself, and is not a "free object". Marx made this point clear when he talked about capital. He said: "Capital is not an object, but a production relation belonging to society and social form of certain periods. The latter is embodied in an object and provides this object with unique social characteristics. Capital is not material or the sum total of production materials." Marx has clearly told us that capital is the existence form and rules of those which exist, and capital's working principles are the constituent principles of modern society. As a general abstract form of existence, capital refers to not only objects' abstract form as social objects, but humans' abstract form as social humans, and even employed workers of capitalists are only personalized capital. As long as we remove the illusion of capital's "neutrality", we can realize the nature of capital and connect the negative influence of capital with its nature. Because capital has necessary negative effects in its manifestation, we should confront, instead of ignoring such negative effects. When we enjoy capital's "benefits", we should also feel various misfortune it brought us. Capital has two basic principles: one is competition and the second is expansion. The two principles' negative results are real and visible. Capital's operation and expansion facilitated production force, increased social wealth substantially, and pushed forward social progress, but this process is immoral in both its power and working mechanism. Because capital's nature is making a profit, capital is the incarnation of greed and horror. Capital's continuous expansion is also a process infringing other people's rights and causing various social contradictions.

In fact, when China is pursuing modernity by using capital, those negative effects determined by the nature of capital and modernity are gradually showing up. In the process of "getting rich", those negative effects might not be so obvious and might be often neglected. But when Chinese people, on the basis of "getting rich", are trying to "get strong", the above negative effects have become prominent and an issue worth noticing. People's target is a system comprising of various goals instead of a single one. In particular historical period, people often stress one goal and neglect other goals; as a result, they often take measures obstructing other goals in order to achieve a particular goal. To "get rich", we must take full advantage of capital, and did not need to think much about capital's harming effects on other goals. Now in our target system, "getting strong" has become the major target; therefore we should not neglect the negative effects of capital, and instead, we should pay attention to them and overcome them.

In the face of these negative effects, we should never make the following choices:

The first choice: Because modernity brought us with difficulties and deprived us of many beautiful things, when we reflect on the life in pre-modern era, we somehow want to abandon our pursuit for modernity and make China a "non-modern holy land" isolated from the world. Some people propose that China should stop the process of westernization and modernization which started at the end of the 1970s. In their viewpoint, since modernity has so many negative effects, we don't we put on the brake in front of the cliff?

The second choice: Modernity is humanity's necessary path of development, and we should walk this path which westerners walked before. Modernity's positive and negative effects are both unavoidable. We can only neglect the negative effects of modernization and walk the original path, and "bathe" the ancient land of China in the waters of westernization and modernization. We can only solve the negative effects when China's modernization is basically completed. And we will disrupt China's modernization process if we try to solve these problems today.

In fact, both choices lead to dead ends. The former requires China to make a turn backward, and the latter will bring China into destruction.

To "get strong', Chinese people must make a third choice, that is to confront and overcome the negative effects.

The so-called "negative effects" mainly include three aspects: Firstly, polarization is getting worse. Today, China is growing in wealth, but most of it ends up in the pocket of a small number of people. 20% of people occupy more than 80% of wealth. While some people rely on modernity and capital to "get rich", others are quickly pushed to the bottom of society. Secondly, the natural environment is getting worse. Accompanying GDP growth is the intensification of the ecological crisis. The serious damage to China's natural environment in recent years is unimaginable. Wherever China's industrialization and modernization are advanced, the destruction of the natural environment will be extended. Thirdly, people are increasingly becoming "one-way" consumer machines. Some people take "consumerism" as their life criterion and concentrate on pursuit for maximization of material interests. Undoubtedly, the gradual elimination of these three negative effects depends on the guidance of Marxism. Marxism is still the main ideological weapon for the Chinese people to understand and solve these problems and contradictions.

For Marx, when talking about modernity, it must be understood in relation to the "capitalist mode of production". Modern society is a capitalist society, and modern civilization is a capitalist civilization. The capitalist mode of production determines the position and historical significance of "modernity" in the evolution of human history. The capitalist mode of production is historical, and modern society and modern civilization are also historical. They formed under certain historical conditions and also will disappear under certain historical conditions. It is inevitable that modern society and modern civilization will be replaced by new society and new civilization. The so-called modernity is the inherent regulations and basic characteristics of modern times. The historical nature of modernity is consistent with that of modern society. Marx regarded "liquidity" as a basic characteristic of modernity. Modernity is indeed a concept of time in Marx, and it is used to express the understanding of the present in historical process. In flowing, historical modernity, existence becomes a "cutting plane" of the moment, a momentary appearance, constant self-criticism and self-abandonment, and "movement" itself , that is, as Marx said, "All newly formed relationships become obsolete before they are fixed."

Marx emphasizes the liquidity and historicity of modernity, and its fundamental purpose is to guide people to surpass it. Marx's basic attitude towards modernity is to realize it, criticize it, and surpass it. In a sense, we criticize modernity in order to surpass it, but achieving modernity also serves the same purpose. Modernity is associated with enlightenment. In fact, Marx began to consider the issue of surpassing modernity as early as around 1845, that is, during his youth. Marx was originally an admirer of enlightenment modernity. Later, he discovered that while enlightenment modernity led people away from worshiping the "sacred image", it also caused people to fall into the worship of the "non-sacred image", that is, commodities, currency and capital worship. Worship of the "sacred image" means that people have not yet gained rationality, while worship of commodities, currency, and capital marks that people have lost themselves again. Marx concluded that under the rule of "non-sacred image", every victory of modernity is a victory of the capitalist class, and the proletariat and the broad masses of working people are lost again. In this way, Marx changed from a pursuer of enlightenment modernity to a critic thereof. Marx, who is the greatest pursuer of modernity, began to have a very sober consciousness: regard surpassing of modernity as the most fundamental and thorough task of mankind. Later, in the field of "criticism of political economy", Marx further expanded his discussion of the above fundamental and thorough task. Certainly, Marx believed that we need to pass through and abandon modernity on the way of surpassing it. The communist society portrayed by Marx for mankind is neither a society of "great harmony" in the old concept and a religious paradise, nor an extreme expression of modern individualism, nor is it to heal with more full and deep modernity the trauma thereof, but the surpassing of modernity.

Marx's concept of modernity is the concept of capital modernity, so Marx believed that humanity will eventually surpass modernity, that is, to surpass capital as the goal of humanity. Marx's criticism of modernity is essentially to eliminate the practical premise and existence foundation of capital in a practical way, that is, to surpass capital. From Marx's point of view, as long as capital is still the basic rules and form of existence no matter what form of discourse is used to criticize modernity and what kind of discourse is used to declare the end of modernity, people have not actually surpassed the historical situation of modernity because of the above fact. At best, it is only self-renovation in "discourse". The liquidity of capital is self-evident. Capital always follows its own trend, leading to the disintegration of all fixed relationships and the elimination of static images. It always destroys everything and changes it. Capital has no boundaries and destroys all boundaries, not only in the extended space, but also in the time of life. The liquidity of modernity is determined by the liquidity of capital. The liquidity of capital and the liquidity of modernity are two aspects of the same process. The flow of modernity and the rigidity of modernity are just the facets of capital. In this sense, the surpassing of modernity depends entirely on the surpassing of capital. In Marx's view, capital can be surpassed. Marx said that the pervasiveness that capital irresistibly pursues will subject it to its own limitations. "These restrictions will make people realize that capital itself is the biggest limitation of this trend when capital develops to a certain stage, thus driving people to use capital itself to eliminate capital." In Marx's view, the necessity and requirement of surpassing capital all come from capital itself. Marx fiercely criticized the cry that capital has no substitute.

Capital has a rationality for its existence in a certain period, but in Marx's view, this rationality does not mean that the existence of capital is eternal and insurmountable, that is, the rationality of the existence of capital in a certain period cannot be used to deduce the eternity of its existence. According to Marx's argument, capital's reasonable existence today does not indicate its existence will remain reasonable forever, that is, it does not mean that it is never insurmountable. Indeed, this position of perpetuating and affirming the rationality of the existence of capital is not related to Marxism. Because Marx is full of confidence that capital will eventually be surpassed, he firmly declared to mankind at the end of the first volume of *Das Kapital*: The monopoly of capital became the shackle of productive force which thrived with and under this monopoly. The concentration of means of production and the socialization of labor have reached a point of incompatibility with their capitalist shell. This shell is about to blow up. The death knell for capitalist private ownership is about to ring. The depriver will be deprived. The Chinese who adhere to the reform and opening-up policy should also have the same beliefs as Marx, and should not shake the belief of exceeding capital because of the rationality of capital's existence in China today. I. Mezaros's book *Beyond Capital* demonstrated the necessity and possibility of human beings to surpass capital under today's historical conditions, and on this basis, it criticized the viewpoint of "no choice" for capitalism and proposed the possibility of mankind to make another choice, i.e. to build a socialist society.

If we focus on how to achieve modernity and how to use capital when we are committed to "getting rich", then we should pay more attention to surpassing modernity and capital when committing to "getting strong". China's true strength must not be entirely based on the realization of modernity and capital utilization, but must be connected with surpassing of modernity and capital. According to the connotation of "getting strong", its basic requirements are far beyond the scope of modernity, and only staying in modernity cannot help us "get strong". The Chinese people determined to make China "strong" must think about how to surpass modernity. Only when the work of surpassing modernity is rolled out can China truly be called a strong country. In fact, the present China, which has basically achieved "getting rich", is fully qualified to surpass modernity and to construct a new form of modernity. First of all, the exploration of modernity in China since modern times has the characteristics of "alternative modernity". The Chinese people originally had the psychological dependence and unconscious choices to learn western modernity on the one hand, and on the other hand they were highly vigilant about western modernity. This complex and contradictory mentality was once described as "the anti-modernity theory of modernity". It can be said that Chinese people already have "cultural genes" that go beyond modernity and pursue "alternative modernity". Secondly, China is committed to the construction of modernization under the banner of socialism. The modernity plan of contemporary China must be placed within the framework of scientific socialism. The value orientation of Marxism determines that China is keeping a high degree of vigilance and refusal toward the general logic of modernity and its inherent disadvantages, and that there is a possibility for China to surpass modernity.

Throughout the process of opening and advancing the path of socialism with Chinese characteristics, we see that this is not only a process of achieving modernity, but also a process that surpasses modernity. The theory of socialism with Chinese characteristics is essentially a theoretical plan for contemporary China to achieve and surpass modernity. It has been suggested that China is actually pursuing a "new modernity" that is different from traditional modernity. This is another way of saying that China is surpassing modernity. The 19th National Congress of the CCP clearly stated that China has entered a new era dedicated to "getting strong". Correspondingly, a series of development strategies and guidelines formulated by the 19th NC also contain factors surpassing modernity. The 19th NC recognized that "the main contradictions in our society have been translated into the contradiction between the people's increasing need for a better life and the unbalanced and inadequate development", and it is our target to fulfill the people's pursuit of a better life. The goal is obviously ultra-modern, which has broken through the materialism and consumerism of modernity, and is close to Marx's requirements for the free and comprehensive development of human beings; the 19th NC of the Party made it clear that the overall layout of the socialist cause with Chinese characteristics is "five in a unity" and the strategic layout is "four comprehensive", emphasizing the comprehensive improvement of material civilization, political civilization, spiritual civilization, social civilization, and ecological civilization, many of which are ultra-modern; the 19th NC of the Party emphasizes the need to adhere to the new development concept, implement the development concept of innovation, coordination, greenness, openness and sharing, and strive to achieve higher quality, more efficient, fairer and more sustainable development. The new development concept is a breakthrough and surpassing of the old modernity development concept; the 19th NC of the Party proposed that the modernization we want to build is the modernization of the harmonious coexistence of man and nature, and the formation of a spatial pattern, industrial structure, production method, and lifestyle that saves resources and protects the environment. We should return to nature the quietness, harmony, and beauty. Such judgments and requirements are by no means confined to modern thinking; the 19th NC of the Party expressed a strong determination to construct a community of shared future for mankind, and proposed to always pursue the road of peaceful development, adopt open strategies of mutual benefit and win-win, adhere to the correct view of justice and benefit, establish a new security concept which is common, comprehensive, cooperative and sustainable, and seek open, innovative, inclusive and mutually beneficial development prospects. Such a world-historical vision and broad bosom is by no means a modern worldview that advocates individualism.

Modernity in Marx's critical theory is a complicated concept. He saw that modernity is bound to be involved in various complex relationships and contradictions, so when discussing the realization and surpassing of modernity, he emphasized that this is a complicated process. Marx's reflection and critique of modernity embodies a deep reflection on the modern rational spirit since the western enlightenment and a revelation of the inherent contradictions of complex modernity.

Some domestic scholars have proposed the term "complex modernity" based on the relevant views of Marx and other scholars studying modernity theory, and based on an examination of the status quo of modernity construction in China today. Around modernity, foreign academics have proposed a series of terms, such as "unfinished modernity" (Habermas), "reflective modernity" (Giddens), "multiple modernity" (Eisenstadt), and "Second Modernity" (Bell). All of these terms include recognition of the complexity of modernity. As mentioned earlier, Marx's research on modernity has a methodological general characteristic, which is to regard modern society as a complex system, and does not consider it as dominated by a single principle. In his view, modernity is also a complex concept. Modern society is a "composite society", which determines that modernity is also a "complex" formed by various factors. The concept of modernity does not exist in a vacuum. As a standardized concept and plan, it is based on a complex living environment. That is to say, the complexity of modernity is the complicated result and experience brought by various contradictions and conflicts in society for a long time. In the "complex" of modernity, "there are both changes

176

in social conditions and social ideas, and the interaction between them makes modernity itself a complicated thing". Corresponding to complexity is simplicity, and modernity obviously has no connection with simplicity. Some scholars put it this way: "Emphasis on the particularity, diversity, and phase and uncertainty (including trial and error) of 'modernity' in space, time, and internal structure are the representation of concepts of 'complex modernity' in historical evolution and contemporary presentation of different cultures." They also proposed that the complexity contained in complex modernity contains "three dimensions": "One is complexity reflected in coordination of norms and self-consistency of internal structure; the second refers to the complexity of conditions and methods of modernity's implementation; the third refers to the development of modernity, namely the generativity and openness shown in its norms and internal structure during implementation."

In fact, we don't need to explain the complexity of modernity as a very complex issue. For Marx, the complexity of modernity is mainly manifested in two aspects: Firstly, the origin of modernity is the same, but the process is not unified. On the one hand, in the process of transition from tradition to modern society, human history has shown the universality of modernity, that is, they are all moving towards the goal of modernity; on the other hand, the national countries of different eras have evolved in their modernization. In the specific display of modernity, it also shows diversity and difference. When Marx discussed modernity, he always showed double examination of cosmopolitan and national nature. The framework of modernity in the perspective of historical materialism embodies the unity of universality and particularity. It can be clearly seen from Marx's exposition that modernity is inherently unitary, while the manifestations of modernity's essence can be diverse. Modernity includes two aspects: "material content" and "social form". From the perspective of "material content", modernity mainly refers to the unprecedented liberation and development of productive forces, triggering profound changes and significant progress in all aspects of social life; and "social form" refers to the way to realize these contents. Obviously, the specific social form of modernity is special and can be varied; but the material content of modernity is universal. Some scholars pointed out: "For the contradictory relationship between the material content of modernity and the social form, Marx once made a concrete and profound interpretation centered on the confrontation between labor and capital." Secondly, modernity is always intertwined with pre-modernity and post-modernity. The nurturing of a modern society from a traditional society was not completed overnight. It is not that the modern society has suddenly replaced the traditional society. With the continuous increase of modernity factors and the decrease of pre-modernity factors, modern society can be established. Judging whether a society has become a modern society depends mainly on whether modernity factors dominate the society, rather than whether the society is permeated with modernity factors. In this way, even if there is a series of pre-modern factors in a modern society, it is normal. On many occasions, Marx has analyzed in detail how pre-modern elements that exist in modern society tenaciously play a role. In the process of constructing modernity, some post-modern elements surpassing modernity will inevitably appear. Post-modernity factors and modernity factors often appear at the same time. In the process of dissolving the pre-modern factors, the expected modernity factors did not appear, but the post-modern factors appeared in front of us. In this way, a modern society must contain pre-modern and post-modern factors.

The process of China's transition from "getting rich" to "getting strong" must be a process of correctly facing and dealing with the complexity of modernity. If the problem of facing and dealing with the complexity of modernity is not very prominent in the process of "getting rich", then it would become exceptionally urgent in the process of "getting strong". The first task required to "get strong" is to scientifically judge the historical position of modernity in China today, that is, on the basis of profound understanding, know how we are involved in the complex contradiction and relationship of modernity. In this way, we can formulate practical measures to deal with such complexity, and realize and surpass modernity. Specifically, we must continue to explore the Chinese-style modernization path which is different from general modernization paths. Since the complexity of modernity lies in the fact that although the goal of modernity and the material content are the same, the ways to achieve modernity are often diverse and different, then we must devote ourselves to creating a Chinese model of modernization. China's "getting rich" depends on this Chinese model of modernization, while "getting strong" depends entirely on whether it can follow the Chinese model of modernization. We must criticize the experience and lessons of modernity in the west, as well as consider China's national conditions; embody the general nature of modernity, and also consider China's special reality; we must abide by the historical development of human society and the development of social history in China. The law must also meet the value demands of human development; the negative drawbacks of modernity must be overcome, and the positive spirit in modernity must be released; the problems in the process of modernity in China must be overcome, and the modernity of China must also be determined. In addition, since the complexity of modernity also shows that modernity is always intertwined with pre-modernity and post-modernity, then for China to "get strong", it must face the entanglement between pre-modernity, modernity, and post-modernity, firmly grasp the initiative to control modernity. As China gradually "becomes strong", the entanglement between the three will become more and more serious. China is "getting strong" in facing, rather than avoiding, such entanglement. When we realize that we should and are committed to surpassing modernity, we must not ignore that there are actually many pre-modern elements in our society. Modernity has not been fully established in China, so we should continue to pay attention to how to use modernity to eliminate pre-modernity. When we focus on how to eliminate traditional elements and establish modernity, we must not forget that on the whole we should put on the agenda how to surpass modernity.

We have repeatedly emphasized earlier that modernity is embedded in the logic of capital. The most urgent task for China today to "get strong" is to correctly face and deal with the complexity of modernity. This is, in the final analysis, to correctly face and deal with the complexity of capital logic. In order to "get strong", we must surpass capital, but capital still plays an irreplaceable role in China today. "Getting strong" is based on "getting rich". "Getting strong" is not a denial of "getting rich", but its sublimation. In order to maintain the foundation of "getting rich", we have to give full play to the function of capital. In this way, we are caught in the complexity of surpassing, restricting, using and developing capital. At present, the complexity of Chinese capital is that we must consider how to make full use of capital to maximize its positive effects, but also how to use capital unlike capitalists in capitalist countries. While using and surpassing capital, we should maintain a reasonable tension between both. So in China today, how to recognize, use, restrict, surpass and reflect on capital has become the key to solving how China can "get strong". With the progress of Marxism's Sinicization, especially with the creative application of Marxist modernity criticism theory combined with China's modernization practice, China is solving the problem of how to "get strong" through the practice of "dominating capital".

VII

The Chinese nation has created a long and splendid civilization and has made great contributions to the development of human society. It was only in modern times that the Chinese civilization was surpassed by the emerging capitalist industrial civilization, and China became the target of the great powers' exploitation and quickly declined. Under the leadership of the CCP, China has progressed from "standing up" to "getting rich". Today, China is moving towards the center of the world stage and turning the great rejuvenation of the Chinese nation into reality. A strong China will have a huge impact on the history of the entire world. What kind of diplomatic philosophy and foreign policy will a strong China pursue? Will it insist on opening-up or return to trade protectionism like the Trump administration in the America? Will it adhere to the principle of independence in dealing with international relations, or export our own social system and culture? Will it continue to adhere to the principle of peaceful coexistence, or has it evolved into a kind of power politics because of the enhancement of national strength? Will it promote common development, or to be the only one, and seek to become the leader and master of the world? Regardless of China's choices, as a strong nation, its diplomacy will affect the future development of mankind. Because China's "getting strong" means rejuvenation of a super civilization, and its world historical influence will be significant and far-reaching. The great rejuvenation of the Chinese nation is essentially a worldwide historical event. It has shaken and will continue to shake the world. The world significance and historical influence of this event have been strongly felt by the world. China seeks to "get strong" not to become a central empire again, nor to prepare to reconstruct a world hegemony system like modern powers. On the contrary, it will surpass not only its own traditions but also modern civilizations through creative transformation of long-term civilizations, and it will open a new way of human existence and international relations. Therefore, a strong China needs true diplomacy of great powers. It needs to be guided by a fundamental idea that penetrates history and reality and have an overall vision of world history. Marxism is such a general theory of world history. Adhering to the guiding position of Marxist world history theory, our international exchanges can form a great pattern and atmosphere, and can closely link the great rejuvenation of the Chinese nation with the progress of human development and make new contributions to the development of human civilization.

The political and economic structure and the pattern of international relations in the contemporary world were established after the Second World War, and led by the United States. In the world structure of the US-Soviet hegemony in the 20th century, it can be said that this structure was not yet universal in the world. After the drastic changes in the Soviet Union and Eastern Europe, the United States became the world's only superpower. The international political and economic order represented by the United States was strengthened, and its values and specific systems were pushed to the world in a peaceful or non-peaceful way. It can be said that since the late 1980s and early 1990s, the world has experienced the process of westernization and Americanization for nearly thirty years. In this process, the trend of globalization has further accelerated. After years of reform and opening up, China finally successfully joined the world trading system. China has therefore become a contributor and beneficiary of world economic development. The global financial crisis in 2008 severely hit the global economy, while China's economy still maintained moderate to high-speed growth, and its contribution rate to the world's economic development was increasing. China has now become the world's second largest economy, and the gap with the United States is gradually narrowing. Against this background, the new president of the United States has set a goal of giving priority to the United States and making the United States great again. It has set off a wave of trade protectionism, fought a trade war, and aimed directly at China. And, under the hype of "China threat theory" and other public opinions, some countries headed by the United States are also creating various hot spots around China to curb China's development. In such a context, what kind of policy China adopts will be very important. Will it adhere to the global integration route of free trade, and persist in opening up, or on the contrary, to implement trade protectionism like the United States, or even come to a full-scale confrontation with the

United States, and return to a closed state in such a competition? We are facing huge historical opportunities and challenges, and it is crucial to correctly grasp the historical development trend, adhere to the correct value goal, and formulate own big country diplomatic strategy in a general world historical perspective.

The 19th NC of the Party solemnly announced that we will further expand reform and opening up, "promoting the formation of a new pattern of comprehensive opening. Opening brings progress, and closure will inevitably lead to a backward state. The door of China will not be closed; instead, it will open wider and wider." We should focus on the Belt and Road Initiative, attach importance to both bringing in and going out, follow the principle of mutual consultation, joint construction and sharing, strengthen innovation and open cooperation, and form an open pattern in which land and sea are linked internally and externally, and east and west can benefit mutually. Meanwhile, we should expand foreign trade, cultivate new trade and business models, promote the construction of a strong trading country, implement a high-level trade and investment liberalization and facilitation policy, fully adopt a pre-access national treatment and negative list management system, relaxing market access substantially, expand the opening of the service industry, and protect foreign investors' legal rights and interests. All enterprises registered in China must be treated equally. We should optimize regional opening layout, further open up the western region, provide free trade pilot zones greater reform autonomy, explore the construction of free trade ports., innovate foreign investment methods, promote international production capacity cooperation, form a global trade, investment, financing, production, and service network, and accelerate the cultivation of new advantages in international economic cooperation and competition". This is a profound interpretation and brand-new development of China's reform and opening policy in the new era. Not only will China not be affected by the conservative trade policies of some countries, but it will form a new pattern of comprehensive reform and opening up both internally and externally. This comprehensive and open strategic choice conforms to the development trend of world history and is a long-term strategic choice and development route. It will have a profound impact on the future development of China and the world. A strong China will seek better development opportunities in the new open world pattern and promote advancement of humanity.

Marxism, born in the middle of the 19th century, has a profound revelation of the overall trend of human development. In the view of the founders of Marxism, the development of human history is the process of the gradual formation and development of the overall world history. Global integration is an inevitable trend of historical development, and no close-door policy can stop this historical trend. In the past, the rule of capitalism was established in Britain and France. Driven by the first industrial revolution, global trade and colonial expansion have just begun. Most countries and regions in the world have not established extensive and close ties, and many places were still awaiting the awakening of commodity capital relations. However, the founders of Marxism have penetrated the trend of the totalization of human existence with their deep insight, revealed the power and mechanism of globalization, and formed the world historical theory in the perspective of historical materialism on the basis of capital criticism. Marx and Engels pointed out that the great industry of capital "created the history of the world, because it made the satisfaction of the needs of each civilized country and everyone in these countries dependent on the entire world, and wiped out the natural closed-door self-preservation state in the past." Due to the capitalist large industry and world trade, "As various interactive activity ranges expand in this development process, modes of production and interaction are improved, the division between various nations naturally arise, and consequently, the original secluded state of various nations thoroughly disappear and our history is gradually becoming a world history." "The state of self-sufficiency and self-seclusion of districts and nations were replaced by their interactions and dependence in many aspects. The same holds true for material and spiritual productions. The spiritual products of various nations have become public property. A partial and limited state of nations have become impossible..." As believed in Marxism, with the expansion of capitalist large industry and global trade, human history has become a generalized world history, and humanity's future development can only be revealed in a globalized and generalized perspective. World history is a generalized human history created in ordinary interactions and connections between humans. The above conclusion belongs to the category of historical materialist ontology and morphology of human civilization instead of the field of history.

Marxism is a generalized liberation theory based on the generalization trend of human development. Therefore, socialism and communism proposed in Marxism on human development is not a theory provided for a specific country or nation. Although the founders of Marxism never opposed to the form of national countries constructed through socialist revolution or the significance of national liberation, Marxism is a generalized theory according to its internal characteristics and principles. It emphasizes the general development and liberation beyond the boundaries of countries and nations. Marxism studies development and liberation in the general interactions and connections around the world and discusses the situation of "humanity". Marx and Engels pointed out that communism can be realized only when it is regarded as a global cause, and it is built on the general development of productive force and world interactions connected to such general development. "Therefore, the proletarian class can only exist in the sense of world history, just as communism can only be realized as a global historical cause. And the global historical existence of individuals means the individual existence directly connected with world history." In *Principles of Communism*, Engels pointed out that communist revolution cannot take place in one country, because "it is a global revolution with activities in a global range." Socialism and communism are by no means a cause limited to nations or countries, and cannot be improved and developed in self-seclusion. Marx and Engels have criticized localized communist much earlier.

Socialism and communism discuss the comprehensive and free development of humans beyond the boundaries of nations and countries. In the final sense, it is not a cause realized by only one country. The opening and reform is an important strategy in socialism with Chinese characteristics, and one of the two basic points of the beginning stage of socialism in China. Following the trend of world history development, the opening and reform policy is a necessary requirement of the global development perspective and an embodiment of Marxist world history theory and human development theory. To follow the Marxist world history theory and human development theory, we must adhere to the opening and reform strategy, integrate into globalization, and influence the social and historical process of globalization with our own strength. Only when we develop socialism in open-minded interaction can we increase socialism's influence and appeal, and attract more people onto this path. Construction in a secluded state is against the historical trend, and cannot help defend or develop socialism. In the new times, we adhere to the opening-up policy and adhere to socialism while reforming and opening the country. This is the objective requirement and embodiment of our adherence to Marxism. Certainly, our reform and opening is conducted based on the socialist path, the guiding position of Marxism and our independence.

Marxist theory is a generalized theory about the general liberation of humans. In essence, it is different from the national democratic revolution theory which focuses on democracy and independence within a national country. Therefore, Mao Zedong called Chinese revolution a new democratic revolution which was different from the old-style capitalist democratic revolution and the socialist revolution in future as imagined by classic authors of Marxism. Mao Zedong thought, as a theory of new democratic revolution is sinicized Marxism and different from the general Marxist theory. The socialism set up through new democratic revolution in China is different from socialism in general and the classic depiction of socialism by Marx and Engels, and it must has its own characteristics. Classic authors of Marxism only, in a general sense, explained the socialist and communist theory of general human liberation. But in actual historical process, Marxist theory is practiced in specific nations and times. Socialist construction and practice in particular countries are always special, and there is no model or pathway applicable for all countries; therefore we cannot impose one particular model or pathway on other countries. While constructing socialism within a national country, we should handle the relationship between countries according to the principle of independence, and this is a basis principle of Marxism as well. In the past, we followed this principle and avoided foreign intervention. After we "get strong", we should still follow this principle, and not impose our pathway on other countries. With our actions, we will prove that all kinds of "China threat theories" and distortions are groundless.

The founders of Marxism resolutely oppose to national exploitation and suppression. Although they emphasize revolutionary alliance and the trend of globalization, they oppose to the act of imposing a nation's will and path on other nations; and they also emphasize independence in revolutionary and development. Marx clearly pointed out: "Enslaving other nations is an act of forging shackles for themselves." In the same sense, Engels also said: "A nation which suppresses other nations cannot be liberated. The force it uses to suppress other nations is finally used against itself." Lenin also had abundant discussions on revolutionary alliance and the relationship between national countries out of the need of revolutionary struggle. He pointed out that because class struggle of proletariat in advanced countries is the top priority, Marx put at the first place the basic principle of internationalism and socialism that a nation which suppresses other nations cannot be liberated. In terms of revolution and liberation, the concept opposing to national suppression and advocating national equality and self-determination means not to impose the pathway of revolution and social development on other nations, or forcibly implant such pathway into other nations. Lenin said: "Marxism always denies artificial launch of revolution, because the progress of revolution depends on how sharp class conflicts are." Lenin also pointed out: "Communism is not indoctrinated with violence." Engels also said: "Victorious proletarian class cannot force other nations to accept any method to increase benefits, otherwise they will lose their victorious position." The principle of independence means that we should defend our own rights; and meanwhile, respect the interests, will and choices of other countries and nations, allow them to choose their own path of revolution and development, and not impose our own will onto them. The diplomatic principle of independence is the basic requirement of Marxist theory.

Of course, socialism and communism promote general liberation of humans and are inclined toward internationalism. But some people abstracted the internationalism advocated in Marxism, oppose to the standing of national countries, and even forcibly interfere with other countries' revolution and construction in the name of internationalism. They regard themselves as world saviors, export revolution to weak countries and imagine they are "doing good". Such behavior violating the principle of independence once seriously affected the relationship between socialist countries and caused various contradictions and conflicts. Great power politics and great party politics once had negative influence on the socialist cause. In the early stage of CCP's founding, it lacked the awareness of independence; it coped the experience and model of October Revolution and caused serious setbacks in Chinese revolution. After continuous exploration, CCP combined Marxism with China's reality, found out a pathway of new democratic revolution different from Russian revolution, and finally gained victory, overthrew the "three big mountains" and led Chinese people to "stand up". In socialist construction, we initially copied the Soviet model, emphasized purity of socialism, and set up a planned economy system of "large in size and collective in nature". After opening and reform, we combined the general theory of socialism with China's backward reality, built up the pathway of socialism with Chinese characteristics and progressed from the stage of "standing up" to "getting rich". History has proved that we must adhere to the principle of independence in both revolution and construction. We can neither copy others' experience nor impose our experience and model on others. We cannot carry out revolution on behalf of others or "bring benefits" for them. Regardless of our experience, pathway and national strength, we should adhere to the principle of independence by not forcing others or replacing their roles.

After the collapse of Soviet Union and drastic changes in Eastern Europe at the end of the 1980s and in the beginning of the 1990s, the world experienced great setback of socialist cause. Some people believed that it was the sign of "collapse" of Marxism and communism. And some people advocated China should take the lead in socialist construction. Faced with complex international and domestic environment, Mr. Deng

Xiaoping refuted the "theory of collapse" of Marxism and communism, and emphasized that if we make great achievement in our own cause, more and more people will believe in Marxism and socialism. On other hand, he emphasized the principle of independence, and that socialist revolution and construction of different countries should be carried out on their own, and we need to respect their choice of their system and development path. By keeping a low profile and not bossing around, we created a good international environment for our construction and development. After decades' development, China substantially increased its national strength and walked into the new era of "getting strong". As a result, some people become arrogant and intoxicated. Does China still need to follow the diplomatic principle of independence after "getting strong"? How do we increase socialism's influence in the world since we made great achievements in socialism with Chinese characteristics? There are some irrational voices on these questions.

In this situation, it is very important to continue our emphasis on the principle of independence. A strong China must have composure, and must adhere to the diplomatic principle of national equality and independence in Marxism. We cannot force our own will or path on others or adopt a chauvinist attitude. The concept of socialism with Chinese characteristics and Chinese Marxism has reflected the principle of particularity in which every country or nation walks their own path, respect each other, remain independent and explore a social development path suitable for their own. Therefore, the proposal of Chinese path itself carries the awareness of particularity, relativity and limitation. The Party's 19th NC report declared solemnly to the world: "China resolutely pursues a peaceful diplomatic policy of independence. We respect other countries' choices of their own development path, defend international justice and fairness, and oppose to the actions of imposing one's will on others, interfering with other countries' internal affairs, and oppressing the weak. China will never develop itself by sacrificing other countries' interests, nor will it forgo its legitimate rights and interests. No country will be able to force China to suffer the bitterness of interest damages."

Since China was invaded by western powers in modern times, the Chinese nation endured great harm by colonialism and power politics. Chinese people know in-depth the cruelty of wars and colonialism, therefore we cherish a peaceful international environment and respect the international relationship principle of fairness and equality. China always follows the peaceful diplomatic policy of independence and oppose to various new and old colonialism, hegemony and power politics. Mr. Deng Xiaoping pointed out: "Socialist China should prove to the world with practice that we object to hegemony, power politics and domination. China is a staunch force maintaining world peace." Walking the pathway of peaceful development is the basic concept of socialism with Chinese characteristics and an essential requirement of Marxism. Marxism objects to all wars and violence of colonialism and hegemony and resolutely defends world peace. In global interactions, the CCP armed with Marxism always adheres to the peaceful diplomatic principle. As the Party's 19th NC report pointed out, the CCP is dedicated to making greater contributions to humanity. "China will raise the flag of peace, development, cooperation and win-win, stay with the diplomatic purpose of maintaining world peace and facilitating joint development, friendly cooperate with other countries based on the Five Principles of Peaceful Coexistence, and push forward construction of new international relations based on mutual respect, fairness, justice, cooperation and win-win."

Marxism objects to and criticizes modern colonial wars and wars seeking hegemony. The international relationship principle of peaceful coexistence has always been the viewpoint of Marxism. There are some misunderstandings and distortions in this regard, as if Marxism is "theory of violence" because it advocates revolution, and as if the relationship between countries is created by strength and wars. In fact, Marxism strongly opposes to wars and prays for peace. Classic authors of Marxism has profoundly revealed the source of modern wars, and objects to imperialist and colonial wars. *Letter to Workers of All Nations* pointed out: "Under the excuse of maintaining power balance of Europe and ethnic dignity, political ambition is again threatening world peace. Workers in France, Germany and Spain! Let's combine our cries into an angry roar against wars! In the workers' view, wars seeking hegemony or defending the interests of a dynasty are totally ridiculous crimes." In the end of the 19th century and beginning of 20th century, capitalist development became more unbalanced, and capitalist powers were involved in fierce battles scrambling for sphere of influence and colonies. The capitalist world progressed from the stage of free capitalism to imperialism, and the First World War finally broke out. Lenin pointed out: "The war at present arose from imperialism. Capitalism has developed to the highest stage. Social productive force and the scale of capital have exceeded the narrow range of single national countries. Consequently, large countries seek dominance over other nations; they fight for colonies as source of materials and site of capital output." According to the theory of classic authors, socialism defends peace, and objects to hegemony and colonial wars. After founding of new China, we regarded prevention of wars and defense of world peace as our basic diplomatic principle.

Since the opening and reform, Mr. Deng Xiaoping put forward that peace and development have become the basic subject of modern times, which was different from Mao Zedong's judgment in his late years. Mr. Deng Xiaoping adhered to the Marxist theory opposing to wars, and repeatedly emphasized China's determination to maintain world peace. He said: "From the political angle, I can make it clear that China is a force maintaining world peace and stability instead of a destructive force. The stronger China becomes, we have more guarantee for world peace." "Our diplomatic policy is to object to hegemony and protect world peace. Striving for peace is our primary task in diplomacy. It is the requirement of people around the world and our construction. We cannot construct our country without a peaceful environment." Besides, Deng Xiaoping connected the principle of peace with socialist system, and put forward that our socialism is peaceful. He pointed out: "Our socialism with Chinese characteristics can continuously develop social productive force and promote peace." Deng Xiaoping actually connected socialist system with the view of maintaining peace and opposing to war. In this viewpoint, socialism should be a force defending world peace.

Of course, Marxism does not oppose to all wars in an abstract way or pray for peace without principles. War can be just or unjust. The war against colonialism, hegemony and fascism is a just war. And the war striving for national liberation and dependence is also a just war. We need strong power to defend peace and justice. Military training aims to prevent wars instead of starting wars. A strong China should, on one hand, adhere to the diplomatic principle of peace; and on the other hand, have a strong capability of preventing wars and gaining victory in wars. We must adhere to a dialectical viewpoint in this regard. A peaceful diplomatic principle does not mean abandoning military training and always displaying weakness. In *Current Problems of Tactics in the Anti-Japanese United Front*, Mao Zedong said: "Struggle is the means to achieve unity, and unity is the purpose of struggle. If we seek unity through struggle, unity can persist, but if we seek unity through concession, we cannot achieve unity at all." The problem of war and peace follows the same principle. If we abandon the means of war and lack the capability of stopping wars, we will also lose the means to protect peace. Only when we have a strong force in military and national defense can we really protect national sovereignty and world peace.

Of course, after "getting strong", we should also prevent arrogance and the "Great Empire" consciousness in feudal times. Only when we maintain a peaceful, humble and rational attitude despite of power can we adhere to the diplomatic policy of independence and make contribution to peaceful development of humanity. Whether a country constitutes a threat to world peace depends not on its power, but on its basic concepts, guidelines and principles in handling international relations. Our country adheres to the pathway of peaceful development and tries its best to contribute to peaceful development of the world. As Xi Jinping pointed out in his speech in the UN headquarter in Geneva on January 18th, 2017, China developed from a weak and poor country into the 2nd largest economy of the world not by means of military expansion or colonial plundering, but by diligence and peaceful work. China will always walk on the path of peaceful development. No matter what stage China progresses into, it will never seek hegemony, expand itself or seek sphere of influence. History has proved and will continue to prove the above fact.

Since the 21st century, the world experienced profound historical changes, and sinicized Marxist theory is faced with a broader global background. After the 19th NC of the Party, our country made huge progress in many fields, socialism with Chinese characteristics has entered a new era, Chinese nation walked into the times of great rejuvenation and "getting strong", and the socialist thought with Chinese characteristics centered on Xi Jinping was developed. Today, China's practice is exhibiting a strong historical influence and facing a broader social and historical stage, and China is bearing a heavier responsibility for world history. In this background, President Xi Jinping explained the concept of a community of shared future for mankind on many important occasions, and put forward the idea of constructing such a global community. The thought of constructing a community of shared future for mankind has produced significant influence in international political practice and attracted the attention of academic circle. Now the thought has been included in the Party Constitution in the 19th NC as the

Party's basic thought. It is an important content of socialism with Chinese characteristics centered on Xi Jinping and an important proposition of Marxism put forth under new historical conditions. In the process of "getting strong", adhering to the guiding position of Marxism and constructing a community of shared future for mankind is the contribution of socialism with Chinese characteristics to humanity's advancement as well as sinicized and modernized Marxism's practical proposal facilitating humanity's advancement under new historical conditions.

Humans' free and comprehensive development is the basic mission and purpose of Marxism. On the basis of modern political liberation, the above purpose has pointed out the new direction of human liberation. Founders of Marxism proposed to overthrow capitalist rule through proletarian revolution, and accomplish general liberation of humans by means of class liberation. A communist society is a brand new form of humans' historical development, and a union of free humans based on their free and comprehensive development in which they can fully realize their free individuality. The communist theory itself is a community theory aiming to achieve general liberation of humans and their free and comprehensive development, and is a great dream for the future of humans. Historical practice after the birth of Marxism told us that it is a long process to realize this great social dream. In this process, we will encounter various difficulties and put forward tasks of the times which need to, and can possibly be solved, therefore we need to put forward symbolic thoughts suitable for the principles and missions of the times. The present era is an era of deepened and quickened globalization, and humanity should cooperate to solve their problems and challenges. Besides, China is more and more deeply connected to the world, making big progress in society and economy, and playing an important role in international affairs. A community of shared future for mankind is a new proposal put forward by considering the basis purpose of Marxism, and analyzing the current social and historical conditions by using Marxist standpoints, viewpoints and methods. This proposal made clear the basic concepts of human development in the 21st century, and won the general recognition by international society. Constructing a community of shared future for mankind is a new task put forward by combining Marxism with the subject of the times under new historical conditions in the 21st century. It is the new mission of Marxism's development in the 21st century, and an important sign of Marxism's development into a new form.

There were many perfect dreams in human society, including the Republic of Plato in ancient times, the universal society put forward by Chinese thinkers, and the conception of Utopia in modern times. However, these dreams lack scientific arguments or solid foundation of practice. Marxism criticized abstract conception of humanity's future, especially utopian socialism, and built up the conception of future society on the foundation of science and practice. Constructing a community of shared future for mankind is a basic proposal of the times put forth according to current social and historical development and the actual situations. It has demonstrated the ideological principle of "being practical and realistic" in historical materialism. On one hand, modern humans are faced with critical challenges, and the above proposal was raised to tackle these realistic challenges. It directly targets the difficult situation in modern times, so it could quickly win public recognition. On the other hand, this proposal was raised based on modern China's national strength and influence, and on the condition that China is more extensively involved in international affairs and bears more international responsibilities. It fits in the changes of domestic and international environment. A community of shared future for mankind is not an abstract concept, but an operable theory with exact practice procedures, development strategy and system conception. The signing of *Paris Agreement*, the proposal of "Belt and Road" initiative, and the holding of various strategic safety meetings are efforts of international society to construct such a community. As the presenter of the proposal, China is making great contribution to constructing the above community through its positive efforts. While constructing the community of shared future for mankind, China should contribute its efforts, share its successful experience, create development opportunities; and meanwhile, it should be practical and realistic, help others according to its capabilities, and stay with the principle of fairness, justice and joint discussion, construction and sharing.

Some schools in foreign theoretical circle, such as new-left and post-modernism, criticize modern society, but cannot put forward a specific plan to change the reality. They cannot put forward an action guideline and basic concept to solve modern humans' fundamental problems, and are displaying a tendency of being more and more radical in thought, but weaker and weaker in practice. Marxist theory is different from the above schools because it is a general, grand narration. Marxism's general criticism of modern society and conception of future development path of humanity have demonstrated general methodological characteristics. In a generalized perspective, Marx gained insight into humanity's general trend of development. In Marx' view, humanity has entered a world history era in which countries and nations depend on and influence each other, and based on their development trend, no one country or nation can remain independent from such a general historical process. Marxist theory itself is a generalized theory analyzing the generality of human existence. Today, the trend of globalization has gone deeper, more comprehensive and thorough than Marx' era. In front of global challenges, no country or nation can remain detached. The Party's 19th NC report pointed out: "No one country can independently tackle the challenges humanity is faced with, and no one country can return to the state of self-seclusion." A community of shared future for mankind is consistent with the general principles of Marxism, the generality of human existence, the general trend of future development, a global perspective and a far historical sight. It has reflected a grand vision and bold spirit. In the process of constructing such a community, it is important to continue with our general thinking pattern and theoretical narration in Marxism.

Marx once pointed out that philosophers are only explaining the world in different ways, and our main duty is to change the world. Practice and revolution are the basic characteristics of Marxism. Marx regarded thoughts and theories as internal elements arising from reality and changing reality. Marxism is filled with subjective spirit which changes reality and pushes forward social historical development. Historical materialism is a subjective historical viewpoint fully demonstrating the social and historical responsibility of creating history. Marxists throughout generations

214

have been the embodiment and practitioners of such subjective spirit. With the change of social and historical conditions, the CCP, as a Marxist governing party, proposed to construct a community of shared future for mankind. This proposal has fully reflected the subjective spirit of Marxism to change history and actively bear historical missions. The thought of constructing a community of shared future for mankind is the full embodiment of Marxist subjective historical viewpoint in the 21st century. This proposal emphasizes humanity's active behavior in historical development, and that history is a progress of self-creation. As President Xi Jinping pointed out in the 95th anniversary of CCP's founding, history has no end and cannot be ended. Only with a strong will of practice can we create history and open new pages of historical development. History is not a spontaneous process dominated by mysterious power, and humans' lives are not destined before their birth. The proposal of constructing a community of shared future for mankind has inherited the subjective spirit of Marxism, is consistent with Marxist subjective historical viewpoint, regards human destiny as our basic mission, and will strongly guide humanity's historical practice in the 21st century. Only when we hold onto the practical and subjective spirit of Marxism in changing reality can we make achievements in the construction of a community of shared future for mankind and make new contributions to humanity's advancement.

VIII

The report of the 19th National Congress of the CCP pointed out: "Socialism with Chinese characteristics has entered a new era. It means that Chinese nation, which has suffered great trials since modern times has achieved the great leap from "standing up" and "getting rich" to "getting strong", and is welcoming the brilliant future of great rejuvenation. It means scientific socialism has shown great vitality in China in the 21st century, and has raised the great banner of socialism with Chinese characteristics in the world. It means the path, theory, system and culture of socialism with Chinese characteristics are continuously developing and have broadened the way for developing countries to modernize, provided new options for countries and nations in the world who wish to accelerate development and maintain their independence, and contributed Chinese wisdom and solutions to solving human problems." The three "means" here indicate a progressive logical structure and connotation. China's process of "getting strong" along the ideological pathway of socialism with Chinese characteristics in the new era is not only associated with the great rejuvenation of the Chinese nation, but also an inevitable extension of the Chinese story since modern times. The global revival in the 21st century is linked to the choice of human modernization. Therefore, China's "getting strong" has world historical significance. As to the formulation of "Contributing Chinese Wisdom and the Chinese Plan to Solve Human Problems" in the report of the 19th National Congress of the CCP, we have to understand the proposal of Mr. Xi Jinping at the 95th Anniversary of the CCP. He pointed out: "We should provide a Chinese plan for humanity's exploration of a better social system." Therefore, to solve human problems, we must rely on a better social system, that is, we must not forget our "initial heart" and "great ideals" of Marxism, scientifically demonstrate the new communist society, and continue to move toward this new society in the practice of the great social revolution. In contemporary China, we should build on the historical process of China's "getting strong" and constantly pursue and display new forms of human civilization.

Relying on the two major discoveries of historical materialism and surplus value theory, Marxism has realized the scientific demonstration of communist ideal society. By summarizing the theories of successive changes in various stages of human society through the historical materialism, especially the detailed analysis of the existing capitalist society through the theory of surplus value, Marxism determined the next development goal of human society -- communism -- based on the regularities of historical movement and contradictions and struggles in present society. The utopian socialists before Marxism, and even the people who have imagined the beautiful society since ancient times, could not understand and explain the reasons and conditions of the historical development status, and at most, they could only conduct some moral, cultural and ideological criticism, even if it was very fierce, they could not find a way to reach the universal society and utopia. In the end, they were often caught in the suspension of a certain moral goal, but in reality they did nothing, or they had a "pastoral idyllic" vision of some pre-capitalist social formations, or even turned to some mysterious fantasy pursuit. But Marx's scientific socialism, first of all, is the abandonment of capitalism. It sees that capitalism is a necessary form for people to carry out their real life under certain conditions, and it is an inevitable stage of people's social and economic form, therefore socialism will be formed under the higher conditions of the times and will inherit the positive achievements of the capitalist civilization.

Marx and Engels scientifically pointed out the inherent contradictions of the capitalist economic movement, and mechanism and inevitability of their economic crisis. The polarization of the rich and the poor in the capitalist society has been repeatedly revealed by the kind people, until once again proved with strong evidence in *21st Century Capital Theory* written by Piketty. The economic crisis of the capitalist society has been recognized by capitalist industrialists, politicians, and scholars. The global financial crisis of 2008 is still haunting the capitalist world. The profound point of Marx is that he not only summarized the two phenomena from the empirical level, but also revealed the inevitable connection that the phenomenal results arose from the basic establishment of productive forces and production relations. Rooted in the "capital labor", the opposite of "man of property and proletariat" polarization, proletariat poverty, as a factor in the economic movement, renders the capitalist market system unable to balance with the rich products provided by the productive force of large industries, which in turn leads to economic contradictions and crises. Consequently, capitalism's value realization and capital's own proliferation have encountered a profound crisis, and capitalism is facing the result of self-denial.

It should be noted that Marxist communism is always targeted, and it is a "good medicine" against the existing social ills of capitalism. It is under the socialist conditions of capitalism that the universal production of wealth must be accompanied by the universal production of poverty. This formed the internal contradictions of the capitalist society, promoted the modern proletarian movement, and also set the theme and fundamental purpose of communism, which is to overcome and resolve the polarization of wealth in a capitalist society, eliminate the resulting social division and confrontation, and realize the free and comprehensive development of people on the basis of extremely abundant social wealth. In this way, Marx and Engels changed socialism from fantasy to science, and it is in this sense that the *Communist Manifesto* asserts that "the demise of the capitalist class and the victory of the proletariat are equally inevitable." In this case, the social forms that Marx and Engels are in and focused on can only be developed capitalist economies such as Western Europe and the United States, and they revealed the objective laws and basic strategies of social revolution. The scientific nature of this road map for social development is itself based on a prosperous and powerful situation in which modernization has been realized and productivity and wealth accumulation are highly developed.

However, unlike the above-mentioned advanced economic and social conditions, the historical situation of China in the modern times was subjected to invasion by western capitalist powers, and was forced to be incorporated into the world historical process led by the west and fundamentally stipulated by the principle of capital. Naturally, the purpose of the western powers' invasion of China was by no means to turn feudal China into a capitalist country, but only to turn China into their semi-colonies and colonies, and to become a peripheral dependency of capitalism. In the process of self-help and rescue of the Chinese people since modern times, the October Revolution sent us Marxism-Leninism. The criticism against capitalism in Marxism, especially the non-capitalist roadmap that Leninism clarified and initially practiced pointed out the basic direction of progress for us. As a latecomer country, we must "learn from Russia", and step through the non-western social form towards a strong civilization. Therefore, on this narrow scale, as stated in the preface of *Critique of Political Economy*: "No social form will perish until all the productive forces that they can accommodate are brought into play, and no new and higher production relationship will appear until the material conditions of its existence mature in the fetuses of the old society." The two "not until" is a profound extension of the two "necessary". It means that the necessity of replacing capitalism with socialism is ultimately determined by the level of productive force development.

The CCP led Chinese people to carry out a new democratic revolution, establish a new China, carry out socialist transformation, and embark on the path of socialism. It sought to establish a new country that broke with its own feudal fetters and was different from the appearance of western capitalism. Therefore, in this sense, Chinese socialism is not "socialism" in the "first stage of communism" in the direct sense of Marx and Engels; it is not a social form "following capitalism", but a development path with comparative advantages "next to capitalism", in the words of Lenin, is to "first use revolutionary means to achieve the prerequisite of reaching this certain level, and then catch up with the people of other countries on the basis of the workers and peasants' regime and the Soviet system." Or according to some researchers, under the premise of backward productivity development level, in the face of the shortage of funds, limited means of accumulation, and the urgent historical task of industrialization and systemic requirements, the Party and the country fully controlled the allocation of resources, ensured high accumulation and gave priority to the development of heavy industry, while at the same time, at a lower level but more fairly guarantee the basic livelihood and social stability of the people.

On the basis of the early exploration of Chinese socialism, the Chinese Communists adhere to the principles of scientific socialism, seek truth from facts, emancipate the mind, and advance with the times, "Boldly absorb and learn from all the achievements of civilization created by human society, absorb and learn from all countries in the world today, including all the advanced management methods and management methods of capitalist developed countries that reflect the laws of modern socialized production" And finally, they developed socialism with Chinese characteristics. As Deng Xiaoping said, reform, as "the second revolution of China", "is the self-improvement of the socialist system, and contains some kind of revolution" Since the reform and opening up, we have completely broken through the traditional socialist social systems based on the planned economy, especially incorporating the market system that has developed in the modern civilization of capitalism into the category of socialism. We set up a socialist market economic system, and transformed it into the basic institutional framework of socialism with Chinese characteristics. We carried out a full range of reforms and institutional system construction in fields of economy, politics, culture, society, ecological civilization and party construction, liberated and developed productive forces in the sense of institutional change and reform, and facilitated the prospering process of contemporary China.

On the path of socialism with Chinese characteristics, we always keep in mind the lofty ideals of communism in Marxism, adhere to the basic system of the Party and country established by new China, regard them as the principles, starting points, the destination and the bottom line that should be maintained, and regard reform as the self-improvement and development of socialism. The Chinese path is rooted in its own historical context and fulfills its essential requirements of "getting rich" and "getting strong". The basic orientation and basic principles of socialism that China has always adhered to are not abstract and empty. "As to socialist principles, the first is to develop production, and the second is to get rich together". This basic principle of socialism is also the basic guiding principle followed by the path of reform and development in contemporary China. Therefore, emancipating and developing the productive forces, together with the elimination of exploitation and polarization, and ultimately achieving common prosperity, constitute the essence of socialism. This scientific definition of the nature of socialism, of course, also pointed out the basic guidance and basic principles for socialism with Chinese characteristics. Precisely, it is the basic line of reform and opening up in the primary stage of socialism -- "Center on economic construction, and adhere to Four Basic Principles and reform and opening up" as abstracted in the 13th NC of the Party. According to Deng Xiaoping's overall design, "the basic line must be followed for a hundred years, and it cannot be shaken." By the middle of the 21st century, we should reach the level of a moderately developed country and basically achieve modernization.

For the beginning stage of socialism, on the one hand, we have the primary nature of the stage, which is constrained by China's economic and social development level, as Marx said in the preamble to the first volume of *Das Kapital*: "Natural development stage", "Can neither be skipped nor canceled by decree", "What countries with more developed industries show to countries with less developed industries is only the future of the latter", Socialist prescription is just "shortening and alleviating the pain of childbirth" as Marx enlightened. Today, the 19th National Congress of the Party formally confirmed to us that socialism with Chinese characteristics has entered a "new era". If we only make intuitive formal logic judgments, then socialism with Chinese characteristics in the new era has not exceeded the "beginning stage of socialism". The report of the 19th National Congress of the Party also clearly stated that "the basic national conditions of the beginning stage of socialism have not changed." However, from the dialectical perspective of the development of the historical movement, the new era also means that the beginning stage of socialism has entered a higher level period and entered the second half, in this sense it has already changed compared with the first half. Moreover, the goal of the second half of the beginning stage of socialism has actually been adjusted beyond the original setting of the theory of "beginning stage of socialism."

Since the 18th National Congress of the Party, as the goal of the first century of struggle tends to be realized, the Party Central Committee with Mr. Xi Jinping at the core, according to the changes in domestic and foreign situations and the development conditions of China, firmly grasp the stage characteristics of China's development. The goals and strategies of China's development and the rejuvenation of the Chinese nation have been adjusted, enriched and improved. First of all, the original plan to achieve the goal of 100 years since the founding of new China, that is, to basically achieve socialist modernization in the year 2035 ahead of schedule; on this basis, he proposed a higher development goal which is to build our country into a prosperous and powerful, democratic, civilized, harmonious and beautiful socialist modernized country by the middle of the 21st century on the basis of basically realizing socialist modernization. Secondly, the development goals of the "two stages" were refined, and the specific goals of basically realizing socialist modernization by 2035 were further clarified: "China's economic strength and scientific and technological strength will rise significantly and rank among the forefront of innovative countries; the people's rights to participate and develop equally will be fully guaranteed; the country, government and society ruled by law will be basically constructed; all aspects of the system will be improved; the modernization of the national governance system and governance capabilities will be basically achieved; the degree of social civilization will reach a new height, and the national cultural soft power will be significantly enhanced; the influence of Chinese culture will be more extensive and deep; people's lives will be more affluent; the proportion of middle-income groups will increase significantly, the gap between urban and rural development and the standard of living of residents will be significantly reduced, and the equalization of basic public services will be basically achieved; the social governance pattern will be basically formed, and the society will be full of vitality, harmony and order; the ecological environment will be basically improved, and the goal of beautiful China will be basically achieved." These goals comprehensively cover the economic, political, cultural, social, ecological civilization and other aspects, which is the refinement, enrichment and improvement of the second goal of century-long struggle.

With regard to the goal of building a powerful socialist modernized country in the middle of the 21st century, the report of the 19th National Congress of the Party further elaborated: "China's material, political, spiritual, social, and ecological civilization will be comprehensively improved to realize modernization of the national governance system and governance capabilities. We will become a country with leading comprehensive national strength and international influence. The common prosperity of all the people will be basically achieved. The Chinese people will enjoy a happier and healthier life. The Chinese nation will stand among all nations of the world with a more high-profile attitude." The 19th NC report put forward the goal of building a strong socialist modernized country. Although it is only one word away from the original goal of the second century --- building a socialist modernized country -- it highlighted that the Chinese nation has ushered in the times when we progress from "getting rich" to "getting strong", and reflected the Party Central Committee centered on Xi Jinping is keeping pace with the times in goal setting and strategic planning. Such a "powerful country" goal has actually exceeded the "beginning stage" standard.

This means that in the process of "getting strong", we will have less and less developed "future scenes" as the goal of catching up with the developed countries. After we "narrate", we need more and more "follow-up talk". Of course, "follow-up talk" is not just a casual talk, but shows that after we have undergone the process of modernization and catch-up development, we are more and more in line with the original plan of the Marxist communist picture. We must promote the Sinicization and modernization of scientific communism under the fundamental guidance of Marxism. In 2013, Mr. Xi Jinping spoke at the 120th anniversary of the birth of Mr. Mao Zedong, "Today, we are engaged in a great struggle with many new historical features." Mr. Xi Jinping's choice to raise this point at this time cannot but arouse our deep reflection, because Mao Zedong once pointed out at the Central Work Conference that was expanded in 1962: "From now on, within 50 years to 100 years, it is a great era in which the social system of the world will undergo radical changes, and an earth-shaking era that cannot be matched by any historical era in the past. In such an era, we must prepare for a great struggle with many different characteristics in the form of the struggle against the past era. For this cause, we must combine the universal truth of Marxism-Leninism with the concrete reality of China's socialist construction and the concrete reality of the future world revolution in the best way possible to understand the objective laws of struggle step by step from practice."

When Mao Zedong discussed the necessity of Sinicization of Marxism, it was precisely that which linked it to the "great era" and the "great struggle" of preparing for new forms and features. Today, Mr. Xi Jinping reiterated the "great struggle". Xi Jinping's new era of socialism with Chinese characteristics has also been brought up at the right time. This is the scientific reflection of the theory on the real historical movement. With its strategic vision and theoretical courage, the new idea accurately positions our prosperity and strength, and reflects our existing achievements and future goals in the grand process of world history. Furthermore, Xi Jinping delivered an important speech at the opening ceremony of the seminar to study and implement the spirit of the 19th National Congress of the Party: "Socialism with Chinese characteristics in the new era is the result of the great social revolution led by our party and the people and is the continuation of the great social revolution". He further elevated the "great struggle" o the height of the "great social revolution". Therefore, just like reform is "the second revolution of China", we can logically conclude that the new era of socialism with Chinese characteristics will launch a "third revolution" in the history of China and the world.

Marx and Engels were not limited to demonstrating communism from a positive standpoint, but with enthusiasm, perseverance, and fruitful refutation, they also dispelled misunderstandings, distortions, and attacks on communism, and China's rich fruit in the process of "standing up", "getting rich" and "getting strong" provided strong evidence for this rebuttal. Especially in the late 1980s and early 1990s, the drastic changes in Eastern Europe and the disintegration of the Soviet Union caused the world socialist movement to suffer unprecedented practical setbacks and fall into a low tide. Correspondingly, it also brought unprecedented theoretical attacks, such as "socialism has failed", "the history of socialism has ended", "socialist regime has been buried in the historical grave" and so on. In the face of the major setbacks of the world socialist movement and the crazy clamor of international capitalism, many people have all kinds of doubts about China. They doubt whether China will follow the footsteps of the Soviet Union and other countries and enter the arms of western capitalism. Fortunately, the Chinese Communists kept a clear head and led the Chinese people to withstand the severe external challenges brought about by the domestic political turmoil and the drastic changes in the Soviet Union and Eastern Europe, and firmly adhered to the bottom line of communism.

Marxism has pronounced the "death penalty" of capitalism, and since Marx and Engels derived the contradiction between themselves based on the premise and operating mechanism set by capitalism itself, as long as we insist on grasping this basic analysis method, it can be clearly judged that the various "new changes" in the capitalist society for more than a hundred years have not changed the finality of the "death penalty" judgment, but only delayed its execution. For example, for a series of new scientific and technological progress and industrial upgrading adjustments in human society in terms of productivity, we cannot look at it from the perspective of use value and think that it has weakened people's resentment and resistance to capitalism. On the contrary, since capitalism itself looks at the problem from the perspective of value, especially surplus value, then without changing the pivotal relationship of "capital - labor" in modern society, the development of productive force will fundamentally aggravate the contradiction with the polarized production relationship and aggravate the economic crisis of relative overproduction, thus making Marx more correct. Reality tells people clearly and ruthlessly: Some new changes in capitalism today have made Marx's diagnosis and judgment of capitalism more convincing and objectively realistic.

Furthermore, the internal confrontation mechanism of capitalist society with economic contradictions as its core hub has also penetrated and eroded all aspects of human society. Especially since the second half of the 20th century, the lifestyles of the entire world have begun to converge, and many people have lived the same life, that is, life marked by consumerism, individualism, realism, and enjoyment. Today, more and more people realize that this kind of life is not what they really expect, and the only way out is to change the current life style stipulated under capitalism and create a new state of existence. As a result, people are increasingly discovering that Marx's criticism of capitalism actually contains the theoretical growth point of the overall criticism of capitalism. Marx's criticism and change of the capitalist production method are not intended to realize in a better way the kind of "human subordination to objects" under capitalism, but to create a new way of life for people. Marx's theory about people's new way of life and the revealing of the world of people's meaning are the guiding light for us to create a new state of human existence.

Marx's blueprint for future communism on the basis of criticizing reality is already a century and a half ago, but mankind has traveled this century and a half, and finally found that we must follow his guidance. Humanity has no choice but to advance communism as their lofty goal.

Moreover, the success of the socialist path with Chinese characteristics confirms the scientific nature of Marxist communist theory step by step. Communism is the fundamental purpose of all theories and practical innovations of socialism with Chinese characteristics, and it is the theoretical weapon for the CCP to lead China to "get strong" in the new historical period. Realistically, as long as you carefully analyze and study the content of the path, system, and theoretical system of socialism with Chinese characteristics, you can find that it not only adheres to the basic principles of Marxism, but also creatively puts forward many new ideas with the orientation of solving practical problems. China practiced many new measures, enriched and developed Marxism, and actually approached communism. In the process of leading China to "stand up", "get rich" and "get strong", the CCP firmly believes that the basic principles of Marxism are unbreakable truths, and that Marxism must be constantly enriched and developed with the development of practice. The CCP led the Chinese people neither to take the old path of closure and rigidity, nor to take the wrong path of changing flags, but to a new path of socialism with Chinese characteristics. The flag of socialism is more and more brilliantly fluttering in China, and socialism is booming with great development. While firmly holding on to the socialist position, China has also rejuvenated the cause of world socialism.

In recent years, as China "gets rich" and gradually shows signs of "getting stronger," political, economic, public opinion, and ideological circles both at home and abroad, have begun to put forward from different positions and understandings a series of connected and differentiated concepts to describe China, such as "China path", "China model" and "Beijing consensus". In the end, the Chinese academic community comes down to the "China path" more uniformly. Firstly, the academic community believes that this title shows that socialism with Chinese characteristics is not static and established, and can highlight dynamic development and future growth. Secondly, the academic community believes that this also appropriately reflects China's objective strength, and its degree of influence on the contemporary world needs to be improved. Of course, we also do not agree to pretend and impose on others, but we believe that with the development of China's path, we must increase the influence of China's path as a contemporary project of scientific socialism. We agree to provide specific styles and detailed pictures of "the model" in this sense.

In the *Communist Manifesto*, Marx made two famous conclusions about how humans should live and what kind of life is meaningful to people. One is that human society must be organized into a "union of free people". The second is that in this union, "the free development of every individual is the condition for the free development of humanity". In a late letter to comrades in the socialist camp, Engels specifically pointed out that no more suitable words could be found to express the main characteristics of the new society. Nowadays, human beings must create a new way of life revolving around this basic idea of Marx and Engels. Creating a new way of life for people includes not only changing the original relationship between individuals and between people and society, establishing a harmonious new relationship between individuals and between people and society, but also rebuilding the relationship between man and nature by transforming the opposition between both into coordination. Marx also enlightened us on what should be the relationship between man and nature and how should this relationship be established. Marx's famous conclusions about shaping nature according to the law of beauty, making nature an extension of human body, and realizing the combination of humanism and naturalism are precisely the guidelines for mankind to eliminate ecological crises and establish an ecological civilization.

The new "great struggle" and new "great social revolution" as a new style of civilization are vividly reflected in the goal of a good life and a beautiful and powerful country, and on the basis of the achievement of "this shore" of "sustaining prosperity and strength", are indicating and partially realizing the "other shore" content of people's free and comprehensive development. Of course, in the primary stage of socialism, humanity's free and comprehensive development can only be partially achieved, but at the same time, we use the living institutional factors of socialism and the subjective factors of the communists and the entire people, to control and guide the direction of economic and social development, serve the fundamental interests of people as laborers, continuously accumulate conditions for the realization of the communist lofty ideals, and continue to move towards the communist lofty ideals including the liberation of man, that is, the complete liberation of labor prescription. We can imitate the sentence of the *Communist Manifesto* to say that in the future, "almost all countries advanced" on the scale of civilization advancement can learn from the scientific socialism of the 21st century by "taking the following measures":

Firstly, we should implement a socialist market economy and make reasonable use of capital factors and principles, but not allow laborers to be the objects of pure capital employment and exploitation. In a foreseeable historical period, the peaceful development of the human civilization community must still be integrated into the global economic system dominated by the principle of capital; especially, countries with low levels of economic and social development need to emphasize the liberation and development of productive force. To mobilize all positive factors and allow free flow of wealth, it is necessary to allow the market to play a decisive role in resource allocation and allow capital to play a positive historical role. But at the same time, the institutional characteristics of socialism have surpassed the state of pure capitalism: the complete separation of labor from the means of production, the free competition in the market, and the existence of an industrial reserve force, making labor only based on its "value", that is, maintain the bottom line of its own reproduction to be purchased by capital. This form of labor commercialization is the way of realizing the opposition of "capital labor" in a capitalist society, and it is a specific method by which capital hires labor and capital surplus value while purchasing labor. Under the conditions of a socialist market economy, we adopt business operations and employment. In such a system, although the institutional mechanism also has the general form of market exchange and contractual freedom, fundamentally speaking, this is first of all to promote the development of modern large-scale production. For the labor force, it also contributes to the transformation of labor, the change of functions and the workers. Therefore, the socialist market economy is the basic form of realizing the limited surpassing of capital and the partial liberation of labor.

Secondly, under the socialist market economy system, in the dynamic balance of labor and labor positions, and in the expansion of the labor production process, the benign growth of the economy and the organic integration of the satisfaction and development of laborers 'material interests are realized. In terms of the basic conditions of the economic social form, only by relying on labor positions can people obtain the necessary means of earning a living, and then develop to a higher level. As far as socialism is concerned, it is necessary to continuously promote the full integration of labor force and labor materials from the internal goals and essence of the system, and to promote the full matching of laborers with appropriate labor positions. In consideration of economic benefits, the socialist market economy also needs to eliminate backward production capacity and reduce labor. However, the socialist system attribute requires that the fundamental interests of laborers are the basis to effectively protect the interests of laborers in the local transformation, and not only the fundamental task of economic growth and productivity development in the primary stage of socialism is meeting the needs of people is not only the process itself, but also the continuous expansion of the labor production process, which needs to constantly absorb the participation of laborers, including laborers who change their positions and upgrade their capabilities as the industry upgrades.

Thirdly, socialism should enable laborers to combine labor tasks and labor processes with the active development of their own life activities after matching corresponding labor positions. From the perspective of Marxism, the development of labor productivity is not only about serving economic output and economic benefits, but also focusing on the improvement of individual workers' material interests, labor compensation and welfare treatment. Socialism enriches people's entire life activities, and continuously improves their subjective ability. Labor is the primary life activity of a person, and the labor position is correspondingly a stage for the display of human life activities. People are matched to a certain stage to engage in labor, which is to rely on it to carry out various activities based on labor. Under the socialist market economy system, we have reconstructed the organizational structure of society, but this does not mean that the enterprise is regarded as a pure economic operating entity and a simple "this shore", it does not mean that it is only paid to workers in monetary remuneration To allow workers to develop their life activities on other occasions and "other shores". Even in the primary stage of socialism, it is still necessary to focus on combining the labor of laborers with the display of their life activities in the process of labor. This combination includes the promotion and development of the social personality of workers.

Fourthly, socialism should promote the ownership of laborers in the labor process and labor organization in an appropriate form of public ownership and social governance system. Marxism believes that the emancipation of labor "is determined by whether the productive forces are owned by the people." Then, the form and degree of realization of this kind of people's ownership also determine the degree of realization of the emancipation of labor. In the gradual exploration and development of the socialist market economy, we have changed the single public-owned economic component of the planned economy era, including the state-owned enterprises, which have also been separated from the mechanical affiliation of state functional departments under the planned system, and have shifted from state assets and capital From an operational perspective, we pursue value preservation and appreciation. Under the new historical conditions and institutional mechanisms, the realization of the master status of laborers needs to go through a more complicated, indirect and detour route. All in all, socialism requires the combination of macro and micro levels in its dynamic development, the combination of the people being the masters of the country and the direct participation of laborers, and the need to give full play to the ownership of laborers in the labor process and labor organization.

Fifth, socialism requires continuous promotion of the formation of joint relations between workers. China's regions differ greatly in terms of economic resources, industrial composition, and level of development. This has also led to the separation of laborers, which in turn has created a complex interest standard and subject. Under the conditions of a capitalist market economy, the profit-seeking nature of capital, the economies of scale, and the inherent impulse to pursue free flow will undoubtedly lead to the spontaneous impulse of disordered competition and blind flow of individual workers following capital investment. Therefore, the socialist market economy requires macro-control and overall coordination. For example, the socialist market economy still requires the proletarian political parties to centralize and unify leadership in the overall political direction, the role of the Party's grassroots organizations as a battle fortress, its cohesion within and across economic organizations, etc.

IX

Engels once clearly pointed out: "Marx's entire world view is not a doctrine, but a method. It does not provide ready-made dogma, but a starting point for further research and methods for such research. In this regard, Lukacs, the founder of western Marxism, once pointed out in *History and Class Consciousness*: "Orthodox Marxism does not mean accepting the results of Marx's research without criticism. It is not about 'belief' in this or that argument, and is not a comment on a certain 'holy' book. On the contrary, orthodoxy in the Marxist question refers only to methods." Reviewing the history of Marxism in China, we will also find that the guidance of Marxism introduced and persisted in China is mainly methodological guidance, which refers to the use of Marxist positions, viewpoints and methods to treat and deal with specific Chinese practical problems, not to say that Marxism provides an existing answer to the problem. It is this targeted and realistic attitude that allows the Chinese Communists to keep pace with the times and be flexible when facing different social and historical tasks at different historical stages. So they are able to master and use Marxist methodology to guide practice. Xi Jinping once pointed out while studying historical materialism in the Political Bureau of the CPC Central Committee: "Marxist philosophy profoundly reveals the general law of the development of the objective world, especially human society, and still has strong vitality in today's era, and is still a powerful ideological weapon to guide the communists." With the ideological weapon of Marxism, our cause can flourish; if we deviate from the basic principles of Marxism, our cause will encounter twists and turns, and even embark on a devious path. As Chinese nation progressed from "standing up" and "getting rich" to "getting strong", it is even more necessary to persevere and develop this powerful ideological weapon to build our country into a powerful, democratic, civilized, harmonious, and beautiful socialist modern power.

To adhere to the guidance of Marxism, we must adhere to the guidance of Marxist worldview and methodology. First, it is necessary to clarify the basic viewpoints and positions of the Marxist philosophical worldview, and adhere to the dialectical historical materialism that Marxism transcends idealism and old materialism. The birth of Marxist philosophy is an important ideological revolution in the history of Western thought. There are different interpretations of this revolutionary change, but the problem is actually not complicated. It is not difficult to see from the ideological background of the birth of Marxist philosophy that on the one hand, the founders of Marxism criticized idealism, affirmed the general principles of materialism, affirmed the material unity of the world, and affirmed that material is the foundation of the world. On the other hand, they criticized the old materialism up to that time, including the materialism of modern natural sciences, Feuerbach's humanistic materialism, etc., that they understand the material world abstractly from historical practice, and they cannot see it. The social and historical nature of the material world after being influenced by human practice also cannot see the material nature of social and historical development. From the perspective of double criticism and double transcendence of idealism and old materialism, Marxist philosophy is a materialist philosophy that surpasses the old materialist philosophy while criticizing idealism. Marxist philosophy has drawn the boundaries of the same idealism, which belongs to the scope of materialism; at the same time, it has drawn the boundaries with the old materialism. The reason why we call this new materialism dialectical historical materialism is because not only social history has become the fundamental research object of Marxist philosophy, but also Marxist philosophy views from a social and historical perspective and on the basis of materialism the unified material world. In social historical practice, people change the subjective world while changing the objective world. The real world is an objective world influenced by human cognition and practice.

Marx once said: "As long as there are humans, natural history and human history restrict each other." People are always in the process of this interaction, and can only understand nature and history from this interactive process. In this interaction, reality is a two-way process in which people change themselves while changing environmental objects. Therefore, Marx said: "The change of the environment and the consistency of human activities or self-change can only be regarded as and reasonably understood as revolutionary practice." Marxism not only understands the development of human history from the perspective of labor practice, but also Criticizing old materialism and historical idealism with this interactive practice concept, criticizing that they cannot understand things and reality in perceptual practical activities, abstracting the real world into a substance that is not affected by the conscious spirit or an abstract spirit without a material basis. Old materialism and idealism are both abstract philosophies separated from practice. Marxist philosophy is based on a practical point of view, criticizing and transcending the metaphysics of these two abstract oppositions. From the perspective of Marxist materialism, the real existence is not an abstract material or abstract spirit at all, but a concrete process unfolding in practical activities. Materialism that departs from practical practice is meaningful for critical idealism, but it is not enough for us to understand reality and social history. We should explain reality and explain things in concrete practical activities and practical relationships, form a correct theory, and guide the practice of changing reality according to the correct theory. In this sense, "the point of view of practice is the primary and basic point of view of all Marxist philosophy, and the category of practice is the core category of the entire system of Marxist philosophy. Only based on the point of view of social practice can we grasp and clarify the Marxist philosophy. The spirit essence can understand and explain the new and dynamic development of Marxist philosophy more than 100 years after its creation".

Marxism does not deny in a practical viewpoint, but has surpassed old materialism. Criticizing idealism, religious theology and feudal superstition from a materialist and atheistic viewpoint is the basic task of modern enlightenment philosophy and enlightenment thoughts. As a critical inheritor of modern enlightenment thoughts, Marxist worldview adheres to, but not remains on the basic standpoint of materialism. For Marx himself, the task of criticizing idealism and religious theology has been completed. And our new task is to reveal the limitations of modern materialism. Marx referred to modern materialism as natural science materialism, mechanical materialism, metaphysical materialism, etc., criticizing these types of materialism for not having a practical point of view, only looking at the material from the material world itself, just seeing the role of nature in history The effect of historical practice on nature cannot be seen. These types of materialism even understand social history in a way that understands the natural world, such as understanding people as machines and society as machines. By criticizing these old types of materialism, Marx and Engels established dialectical historical materialism based on practical viewpoints. Historical materialism looks at the world from a practical and historical perspective, and believes that the world is no longer an abstract and free material world, but a realistic process unfolding in the material world that transcends the natural and historical integration of the material world. The "material" in historical materialism no longer refers only to the substance in the sense of the old materialism, but the actual relationship, mode, structure and process of existence of practical intermediation. In this sense, social existence becomes the basic category of historical materialism, social existence determines that social consciousness becomes the basic principle of historical materialism, and historical materialism becomes a new stage and form in the development history of materialism.

Analysis of the limitations of old materialism is not unique to Marxism. Engels once quoted Feuerbach as saying that Feuerbach also knows that the logic of the natural material world cannot be used to understand human history, and the existence and development of human history has its particularity. However, Feuerbach, aware of this difference, used love and religious emotions to explain historical development. Marx and Engels, like Feuerbach, criticized the old materialism using the logic of the natural material world to understand the vulgar materialism caused by history, while also criticizing Feuerbach's understanding of historical idealism from the internal spiritual factors. Historical materialism understands history from a practical point of view, emphasizes the unity of the interaction between natural history and historical nature in practice, and criticizes the abstract opposition that separates nature from history. The Marxist view of history is a materialistic view of history based on practice. History is not a process of unfolding according to the inevitability of nature, nor a process of voluntarism based on the subjective will of human beings, but the interaction between subject and object in practice The product is a dialectical process in which the economic foundation determines the superstructure and the superstructure reacts to the economic foundation. Based on this basic viewpoint and basic principles, historical materialism has formed a series of historical viewpoints that are different from the old materialism and historical idealism.

The historical view of historical materialism is the core of Marxist philosophy. Engels once said that the historical view of materialism is one of Marx's two important discoveries. The historical view of historical materialism criticizes the historical view of old materialism and idealism at the same time: Criticizing old materialism can not see the particularity of history, and understand history from the perspective of the material world; critical historical idealism interprets history from the concept and spirit, Fall into subjectivism. Based on practical viewpoints, historical materialism breaks the abstract opposition between objectivity and subjectivity and forms a series of methodological principles for understanding history. To adhere to the guidance of the Marxist methodology is to adhere to these basic principles in theory and practice, the first of which is the ideological line of being practical and realistic.

This year marks the 40th anniversary of reform and opening up, and the 40th anniversary of the publication of "Practice is the only standard for testing truth." From the central government to local governments, from theoretical propaganda departments to academic research institutes, there has been an upsurge to commemorate the reform and opening up and the discussion of standards of truth. It was the discussion of standards of truth that blew the clarion call for reform and opening up, and since then Chinese society has been completely renewed and has entered a new period of building socialism with Chinese characteristics. After 40 years of construction and development, Chinese society has undergone tremendous changes, from "standing up" into the era of "getting rich". Through reform and opening up, the second historical leap from Mao Zedong Thought to Deng Xiaoping Theory took place in the course of Marxism in China. Today, with the all-round development of my country's social and economic construction, and the changes in the main contradictions of Chinese society, Chinese society has moved from "getting rich" to a new era of "getting strong". The new era has spawned new ideas, and the third historic leap in Marxism in China is taking place. Xi Jinping's socialism with Chinese characteristics in the new era is playing a powerful role, becoming the spiritual force guiding the practice of building socialism with Chinese characteristics in the new era, and the common national will in the new journey of the great rejuvenation of the Chinese nation. This is an era of advancing and advancing with the times. In the new era, it is important to reaffirm and uphold the basic Marxist ideological line of being practical and realistic. It allows us to avoid making mistakes of subjectivism and dogmatism in the new journey of "getting strong", truly combine theory with practice, ideals with reality, and without boosting and exaggeration, push forward the process of great rejuvenation of Chinese nation in a down-to-earth manner.

Practice is the fundamental viewpoint of Marxist philosophy. Theory comes from practice, and at the same time it is tested and developed in the process of guiding practice. The relationship between theory and practice is a mutual regulation and mutual promotion. This requires us to adhere to the ideological line of being practical and realistic. Correct thoughts and theories can only come from objective studies of reality, rather than absolute dogma and absolute principles that deviate from specific social and historical conditions. Only correct theories that meet the real situation can bring correct practice. In the article *Reshaping Our Learning*, Mr. Mao Zedong emphasized that the attitude of being practical and realistic "is to study Marxist-Leninist theories in a targeted manner, combine the theory of Marxism-Leninism with the actual movement of the Chinese revolution, and find positions, points of view, and methods in the theory to solve the theoretical and strategic problems of the Chinese revolution." He also called the attitude of "being practical and realistic" as the attitude of "shooting the arrow at the target". "Chinese Communists are looking for this 'arrow' to shoot the 'target' of Chinese revolution and oriental revolution." Being practical and realistic means to study the internal relations of all things that exist objectively, study the regularity, and form a correct theory to guide practical practice. Only by adhering to the ideological line of being practical and realistic can we avoid a subjective attitude, avoid the dogmatism which neglects Chinese reality and facts, and truly achieve the dialectical unity of theory and practice. Mao Zedong said: "Our conclusion is the specific historical unity of subjectivity and objectivity, theory and practice, knowledge and action, and we oppose any 'left' or 'right' thinking patterns deviating from actual history." Being practical and realistic is Mao Zedong's summary of the Marxist ideological line in China. Deng Xiaoping said: "Marx and Engels created the ideological lines of dialectical materialism and historical materialism. Mao Zedong summarized in Chinese language with the four characters 'Shi Shi Qiu Shi', meaning being practical and realistic. We proceed from reality, integrate theory with practice, and insisting on the principle that practice is the standard for testing truth. This is the ideological line of our Party. ... This ideological line of the Party was established by Mr. Mao Zedong. He has adhered to this ideological line for most of the times when he led revolution."

The thought principle of being practical and realistic is the key and precious experience of China's success in revolution, construction and reform. In the process of Marxism's Sinicization, whenever we could adhere to this thought principle and properly deal with the relationship between general Marxist theory and China's reality, whenever we developed smoothly in our causes. On the contrary, whenever we deviated from this thought principle and embraced dogmatism, subjectivism or empiricism, we suffered setbacks or disastrous blow in our causes. The same held true in both the period of revolution and peaceful construction. Although we made astonishing achievements during socialist construction, the "great leap forward", "catching up with Britain and America", and the "cultural revolution" having lasted 10 years brought about severe disasters for socialist construction. Since the Third Plenary Session of the 11th Central Committee of the CCP, Deng Xiaoping, the chief designer of opening and reform led the Party and Chinese people to set things right, objectively evaluate Mr. Mao Zedong's historical merits and mistakes in late years, restore the thought principle of being practical and realistic through the major debate on truth standards, and open a new era of socialist construction with Chinese characteristics. Deng

Xiaoping pointed out: "Being practical and realistic is the basis of proletarian worldview and Marxism. We gained victory in revolution by following this principle. Now we are headed for the purpose of Four Modernizations; and still, we should follow the above principle." Based on the thought principle of being practical and realistic, we made a basic judgment that China is and will be, in the long term, positioned at the beginning stage of socialism, and changed the previous judgment on war and revolution based on the times. We put forward that peace and development are the basic subjects of modern times. On this basis, we put forward the basic pathway for the beginning stage of socialism -- "one center and two basic points" -- and the strategic "two steps". Under the guidance of Deng Xiaoping theory, Chinese society completed the great journey from "standing up" to "getting rich".

Adhering to the thought principle of being practical and realistic is an excellent tradition of our Party. Only by following this thought principle can we form a correct theory to guide realistic practice. President Xi Jinping pointed out in the report of the 19th National Congress of Party: "Since the 18th National Congress of the Communist Party, changes of the situation at home and abroad and the development of various undertakings in China have brought us a major topic of the times. What kind of socialism with Chinese characteristics we should adhere to and develop in the new era, and how to adhere to and develop socialism with Chinese characteristics, including the general goals, tasks, overall layout, strategic layout and development direction, development mode, development motivation, strategic steps, external conditions, political guarantees and other basic issues for developing socialism with Chinese characteristics in the new era, and according to new practices, we should provide theoretical analysis and policy guidelines on economics, politics, the rule of law, science and technology, culture, education, people's livelihood, ethnicity, religion, society, ecological civilization, national security, national defense and military, 'one country, two systems' and the motherland's unity, united front, diplomacy, and Party construction in order to better adhere to and develop socialism with Chinese characteristics." Centering on this major subject of the times, our Party "adheres to the principles of liberating thoughts, being practical and realistic, keeping pace with the times, and being pragmatic, follows the path of dialectical materialism and historical materialism, and by considering new conditions and practical requirements of the times, deepens our understandings of the CCP's governing rule, socialist construction rule and human society development rule from a brand new vision, carries out arduous theoretical exploration, and has made great theoretical innovation, and created socialist thought with Chinese characteristics in the new times." The thought principle of being practical and realistic is permeated through socialism with Chinese characteristics in the Xi Jinping's times. Socialism with Chinese characteristics has included the above thought principle as its basic requirement, and it is also a reflection of the Party's adherence to the above thought principle. Socialism with Chinese characteristics in the Xi Jinping's times was formed by liberating thoughts, being practical and realistic, and applying and developing Marxism based on changes of historical conditions in China and overseas and the characteristics of the times. The above socialist thought is the latest result of Marxism's Sinicization, and the basic content of Chinese Marxism in the 21st century.

Today, Chinese nation progressed from "getting rich" to "getting strong". At this time, we should adhere to the thought principle of being practical and realistic, properly grasp the pulse of the times, objectively evaluate our achievements, and rationally set out goals for the future. We should, on one hand, be self-confident, and on the other hand, avoid being boastful; we must hold a down-to-earth, humble, cautious, and diligent attitude, construct socialism with Chinese characteristics with our action, answer the questions of the times with real achievements, and win the world's respect with our virtues of humility and gentleness.

Being practical and realistic is the basic ideological line of Marxism and the basic line of understanding formed by the CCP in the course of long-term revolutionary practice. This line has played a very important role in guiding China's revolutionary construction and reform practice. However, we cannot misunderstand the ideological connotation of this line. The theoretical connotation of this ideological line can only be deeply understood on the basis of the concept of historical materialist practice. This ideological line can neither be understood as an empirical proposition, nor as an positivist proposition. In other words, adherence to the ideological line of being practical and realistic must be linked to adherence to historical materialism and adherence to the historical analysis method based on practice. Viewed as a dogma that precedes practice and therefore prescribes practice. Historical materialism sees reality as a historically unfolding process in which theory and practice are dialectically unified, so it insists on looking at problems with historical eyes. Historicity is the basic methodological principle of historical materialism. It requires looking at things with a historical development perspective and grasping things in the overall development of history. Adhering to the ideological line of being practical and realistic at the same time means adhering to the Marxist historical analysis method, because "practice" is not an object that does not change, and "reality" is not an abstract rule that does not change.

The basic feature of dialectics is to look at problems with a connection and development perspective. The question is how to look at connections and development. Hegelian philosophy is the master of classical dialectics. He emphasized that truth is the whole and the process. The viewpoint of connection and development is fully reflected in this proposition. Hegel's philosophy is a science that studies the inevitable connection and development between categories and categories, and Hegel's philosophy also explains the basic categories and basic laws of connections and development itself. Contrary to Hegel's idealism, modern materialism also talks about connection and development, and changes in movement, but they basically understand the connection and development of the world with mechanical physical movement patterns, thinking that animals are machines, even humans are machines. Social Darwinism also uses the perspective of biological evolution to understand connections and development, and the movement of social history according to the model of biological organisms. How do we understand the connection and development in reality in Marxist philosophy? Has it reversed idealism and therefore interpret the world as a free material movement process like modern materialism? In short, what are the fundamental characteristics of Marxist dialectics? Does the "reality" mentioned in "being practical and realistic" refer to the material world itself that moves freely? Does the "practice" sought in "being practical and realistic" only refer to the law of causality in the material world? Is "being practical and realistic" a kind of epistemological view of mechanical reflection theory? This is clearly not the fact.

Marxist dialectics is founded on practice. It does not analyze the connection and development of objects in a general way, but interpret the movement, development and change of objects in historical practice. Therefore, it is different from the idealist dialectics and has surpassed the dialectics in old materialism. In the visual field of historical materialism, the process of connection and development does not only refer to the spontaneous connection and development within and between objects, but the process of connection and development under the influence of human practice in humans' survival activities. This process is always connected with humans' historical practice, therefore it is a social and historical process influenced by humans' subjective elements. The same object may display different connotations, functions, values and significance in different social historical relations. We cannot understand objects in an abstract way detached from specific social historical relations, as if understandings are intended to provide an absolute truth and general principle surpassing social and historical time and space, and we can apply these truths and general principles to everything in the world. This is a dogmatic attitude of persons who do not understand Marxist historical analysis. Marxist historical analysis requires us to carry out concrete analysis of objects based on practical requirements under specific social historical conditions, and understand the special rules of objects and phenomena.

It is first emphasized in historical analysis that we should understand objects in social historical relations created by practice, and make clear the specific relationship between objects and phenomena and humans' practical activities. The specific nature of practical activities has determined the special relation between objects and phenomena and humanity, the relativity and limitation of understandings, and that such relativity and limitation will not cause relativism and nihilism. Because objects' quality, state and function are relatively fixed in certain social practical context, our understanding of objects must be true or false, right or wrong, and our evaluation of objects may be positive or negative. Because of the emphasis on practicality, the historical analysis method also emphasizes looking at objects with a developmental perspective. Human practice always changes the subjective world of humans while changing the objects, the dialectical relationship between the subjective world and the objective world, and promotes the development and change of reality. Therefore, historical materialism opposes the view that the world and reason does not change. It advocates looking at objects with a development perspective, and emancipating the mind, adapting to the times, and advancing with the times. These points of view are full manifestations of historical analysis. Persisting in looking at problems with this development perspective, we can "be brave in reform and innovation, never stagnate and never be rigid", and be determined to forge ahead and stay young.

Classic Marxist authors always emphasize the use of developmental perspective to look at objects, and oppose to all pretentious, conservative and rigid attitudes. Marx once said: "What should be done at a specific moment in the future, and what should be done immediately depend entirely on the established historical environment in which people will have to operate." In Marxism, we not only look at objects in the developmental perspective, but also look at Marxist theory itself in the same way. Engels once clearly pointed out that Marx's whole world view "provides not a ready dogma, but a starting point for further research and methods for such research". It is with this developmental perspective that Marxism itself can keep pace with the times and become vibrant. A strong China must adhere to the historical analysis of Marxism, keep pace with the times, and prevent all kinds of rigidity and conservatism.

Marxist theory is the product of human beings moving towards the era of world history. The founder of Marxism was an encyclopedic writer, synthesizing the basic achievements of the main scientific developments of the time, and creating a huge overall system that was integrated. In terms of the time background, Marxism is the product of human civilization moving towards global integration. What we consider and study is the totality of human existence, as a whole of human society and human history. In terms of specific content, Marxism is a general theory having realized comprehensive innovation of multiple disciplines. Especially from a methodological point of view, Marxism runs through a dialectical historical general consciousness and insists on using dialectical generalized thinking to understand objects and grasp reality, so it can become the essence of the spirit of the times. Adherence to dialectical general awareness is an important principle of Marxist methodology. In the face of contemporary reality and ideological context, on the one hand, it is the acceleration of the deepening of global integration, on the other hand, it is the broad influence of post-modernism that advocates micro-narratives and opposes general thinking, and adheres to and highlights the dialectical generalized thinking mode. It is crucial for us, a big Party that leads more than 1.3 billion Chinese people to national rejuvenation. Only by having a generalized mindset, considering the overall situation and looking forward, can we "improve our strategic thinking ability, comprehensive decision-making ability, and control the overall ability, and unite and lead the people to continuously write a new chapter in the history of reform and opening up."

In the view of some postmodernists, totality is an inherent feature of the grand narrative of modernist theory, which reflects the expansion and "overstepping" of human beings as modern subjects in theory and practice without boundaries. In general, postmodernism carefully avoids absolute values, solid epistemological foundations, overall political vision, grand theories about history, and "closed" conceptual systems, which are skeptical, open, relativistic, and pluralistic, praising division rather than coordination, fragmentation rather than wholeness, heterogeneity rather than unity, it sees the self as multifaceted, fluid, temporary, and unity without any substantial whole. Postmodernism advocates a small narrative and micro-narrative. Some postmodernist theorists believe that modern total narrative is the ideological root of totalitarianism and authoritarianism, which has led to disasters in the practice of modern society. In their view, Marxist theory is not only the successor of modernity theory but also its most extreme form. Under the banner of opposing and criticizing the overall narrative, Marxism has become an important object of postmodernist criticism.

Indeed, from a variety of perspectives, Marxist theory has significant overall characteristics. The overall characteristics of Marx's critical theory embodies the internal ideological logic and the unity between theory and practice. It should be said that this is difficult to be achieved by the theoretical research and the fragmented ideas of contemporary disciplines. This total narrative is not based on the abstract totality of metaphysics, nor does it necessarily lead to practical authoritarianism and exclusivism. The general characteristics of Marx's critical theory cannot be simply equated with abstract identity thinking, or even the totality in Hegel's conceptual speculative connection. Marx emphasized understanding the nature and meaning of specific, special, and differences in the overall connection between historical practice and social relations. Only in the connection and development of social history can we truly grasp the specifics, specialties and differences. The history and society as a whole are not regarded as static. This kind of holistic thinking can avoid raising "individual", "special", "difference" and "plurality" to the absolute level, and avoid falling into "special" tyranny and exclusivity. Criticizing the totality of abstraction, defending differences, pluralism, speciality, concreteness, etc., but not excluding the totality narrative itself in an abstract manner, and not giving up the overall way of thinking. The specificity of specific things can only be correctly understood in the historical totality.

It requires a strong capability of abstraction, totality thinking and a grand theoretical attitude to accurately understand the trend and internal principles of historical development. We cannot follow the steps of shallow post-modernists to object to and abandon the totality method. In this sense, Lukacs once pointed out that the totality view of dialectics is the only means to reproduce and understand reality in our thinking. If we abandon the totality method, we can never form a reasonable concept of times and history in pure concrete objects. In fact, as a means of human thinking, totality thinking is not necessarily opposed to specificity, difference, tolerance and diversity. The totality thinking in Marxism does not deny specificity and difference, and it is fundamentally wrong to equate totality thinking to metaphysical thinking or political autocracy: Firstly, totality is regarded as abstract identity and placed in conflict with specificity. In fact, abstract totality may cause absolutism and exclusionism, and in abstract specificity, such a possibility increased instead of reducing. Because specificity may fall into abstraction, abstract specificity detached from totality is abstraction itself. Marxist totality thinking emphasizes historical unity between specific and total dialectics instead of placing the two in conflicting positions. Secondly, this is a kind of conceptualism. It does not include the connection between the way of thinking and the theoretical characteristics and the existence of history. It seems that overall thinking is rooted in people's internal concepts. The capitalist mode of production is the intrinsic driving force of the modernization of the modern world. Only in such a world historical era as the modern era, the overall concept of time and history is realistic. In other words, the reason why Marxist totality theory and totality thinking is possible is precisely the product of the development of modern history. Thirdly, this is a non-reflective review of the problems in practice to the theory, which directly corresponds to authoritarianism and totalitarianism and concepts, without seeing the accidental and specific factors in the specific history, and the thought and practice The complex process between multiples, reducing the simplicity of practice to thought, is an idealist position. Fourth, this is the question of human rational knowledge and self-creation ability caused by the enlightenment of the subjective appeal after the destruction of contemporary reality. In fact, without grasping the totality of modern history, you will be lost in the scattered and disordered differences and pluralism, and "modernity" will become an uncontrollable "free object" and will be pushed into the infinite darkness, It will even be criticized as a total conceptual abstraction with no methodological significance. Therefore, we need to criticize the abstract totality or identity thinking, but we should not oppose the abstract totality with abstract concrete. Marxist totality thinking is a dialectical totality method connected with the principle of being practical and realistic and historical analysis, and it is the dialectical unity of specificity and totality.

Marxism emphasizes being practical and realistic, and viewing and understanding problems in a connective and developmental vision. Therefore, Marxist totality thinking is neither metaphysical abstract identity nor the sum or synthesis of various parts and elements, but requires understanding of objects in the general connection and process of social and historical movement; therefore it can always penetrate the nature of objects, predict historical development trend, form a macroscopic understanding of reality, and become a strong thought leading reality. We are a large Party with more than 80 million members, and we are constructing socialism and rejuvenating the nation in such a large country with a long history, large population and vast territory. Without a totality thinking pattern which looks into the future, grasps the general situation, and devise overall strategies, we cannot make a success. Xi Jinping pointed out: "Our Party is faced with a very complex domestic and international environment and bearing heavy missions of governance while governing such a large country with a 1.3 billion population. Without the strong support of theoretical thinking, we cannot overcome various risks and difficulties and move forward continuously. The Party leaders, especially senior cadres, should study classic works as they are, and use Marxist philosophy as their special skill. By adhering to our ideal faith and the correct political direction, and enhancing our capability of strategic thinking, decision-making and overall management, we will lead the people to write a new chapter in opening and reform." President Xi Jinping emphasized the dialectical totality thinking pattern in Marxism. Only by adhering to and effectively using such an advanced art of thinking can we "govern the large country like preparing a meal." Only when we adhere to such a totality thinking pattern can we understand the historical orientation and significance of socialism with Chinese characteristics in the new times in a macroscopic vision of historical development, and make a realistic and objective judgment: "The entry of socialism with Chinese characteristics into the new era has great significance in the development history of the People's Republic of China, the Chinese nation, world socialism and human society. Our Party should build up self-confidence, work diligently, and enable socialism with Chinese characteristics to demonstrate stronger vitality!"

X

In the previous chapters, we explained that Marxism has been a strong spiritual force and thought weapon during the great rejuvenation of Chinese nation. In the past, we "stood up" and "got rich" under Marxist guidance, and in the new times when we progress from "getting rich" to "getting strong" and construct a socialist modernized strong country characterized by wealth, democracy, civilization, harmony and beauty, we should still, and with more determination, adhere to the guidance of Marxism. Only by adhering to Marxism's guiding position in constructive causes and the direction of sinicized Marxism can we realize the great rejuvenation of Chinese nation. Theory and practice complement each other. Proper theory is the flag guiding practice, and rich practice is the soil testing and nurturing theory. As the Party's 19th NC report pointed out: "The times is the mother of thought, and practice is the source of theory. As long as we listen to the voice of the times and are brave enough to stay with the truth and correct our mistakes, Marxism in China of the 21st century will certainly demonstrate strong and pervasive power of truth." We are not meant to be dogmatic Marxists. While guiding practice with Marxism's basic standpoint, viewpoint and methods, we should, as part of Marxism's Sinicization, enrich and develop Marxism, provide it with a new image of the times, and lift it to a new historical height. A strong China will play a huge role in Marxism's Sinicization and modernization, and make important contribution to the development of Marxism and socialism. As Chinese Marxism in the 21st century, the socialist thought with Chinese characteristics in the Xi Jinping's times will push Marxism into a new historical stage. Here, we will explain the innovation and development of Marxist theory in the form of Chinese Marxism in the 21st century by studying socialist thought with Chinese characteristics in the Xi Jinping's times.

The concept of a community of shared future for mankind has demonstrated the general human standpoint hidden in the class discourse of classic authors of Marxism. And the responsibility for general destiny of humanity has been directly stipulated as the mission of modern Marxism.

As we know, modern times are called the era of subjectivity and the era of humanism. The liberation of human beings is the basic connotation of modern concepts. However, the subject in modern liberation theory is the subject of abstract identity, that is, the atomic individual with the abstract rights as the core. The liberation of the subject refers to the individual's obtaining abstract rights that are not restricted by their social relations and status. The natural human rights theory in modern political philosophy, the economic man hypothesis in economics, and the self-awareness in philosophy are all theoretical expressions of modern subjectivity. Marx theoretically criticized this concept of abstract subjective liberation, and revealed the actual differentiation and opposition between people through the analysis of production relations. Class analysis and class liberation have become the basic content of Marxist theory. Marx criticized that modern liberation is only political liberation, not the liberation of all areas of life, but the liberation of the proletarians to become rulers and to gain dominance, but not to all people. The human liberation envisioned by Marx is the total liberation of mankind achieved in the form of proletarian liberation, not only for all people, but also for all areas of life. It is in this sense that Marxism is the theory of the liberation of the proletariat, and at the same time it is the theory of the realization of the total liberation of mankind in the way of class liberation.

In other words, the theoretical purpose of Marxist proletarian liberation is not just the liberation of the proletariat itself, nor is it that the proletariat becomes a new depriver after it deprives the depriver. The mission of class liberation is to eliminate the social and historical conditions of class existence and class rule. Therefore, it is necessary to establish a human community free from exploitation and oppression, that is, the union of free people that Marx mentioned. Marxist theory of class liberation is actually a community theory of the total liberation of mankind and the realization of humans' free union. Marx's class standing itself reflects the overall standing of mankind. It is not real Marxism to use Marx' class standing to deny Marx' human standing, or conversely, use human standing to deny Marx' class standing and fall into an opposition between one and the other. The proletariat cannot liberate humanity if it cannot liberate themselves. Similarly, if the proletariat cannot liberate the humanity, it cannot liberate itself. This is a historical process of dialectical unification. Marx criticized the capitalist mode of production from the perspective of class analysis, and revealed class exploitation and class oppression. This in no way means that Marx' theory is just a theory about class liberation, and it does not have the meaning of general human liberation. If we start from a narrow class standing against human liberation, we could not understand the human orientation of Marxist theory, the historical mission and responsibility of Marxism to liberate all mankind, or the general meaning of Marx' capital critique in a broader sense.

It seems today that the development of modern civilization based on capitalist production methods has encountered an unprecedented dilemma. This dilemma refers not only to the exploitation of the proletariat, but also to the difficulty of sustaining human existence itself. The contradictions between the classes, the contradictions between the countries, and the contradiction between society and nature are all directly related to the capitalist mode of production and the civilized form prescribed by it. The grabbing and utilization of natural resources by capital has promoted the development of social production and brought a crisis of human survival. Mankind has increasingly become a stakeholder community of destiny, and human survival is facing unprecedented crises and challenges. Under such historical conditions, building a community of human destiny has become the fundamental theme of today's era and the fundamental task that determines the future of humanity. This important proposition in Xi Jinping's socialist thinking with Chinese characteristics in the new era highlights the overall position of mankind on the basis of traditional Marxist class narratives and innovates the theoretical expression of Marxism. This proposition cuts into the basic theme of today 's era. It can incorporate more social practice into the theoretical horizon of Marxism, and at the same time, it can start a critical dialogue with some non-Marxist theoretical perspectives, so that Marxism can go with the times and be able to Leading the development of

287

the times, showing the contemporary significance and historical role of Marxist theory.

Combined with today's reality, the idea of constructing a community of shared future for mankind combines the realization of the free and comprehensive development of mankind with the mission of salvation that sustains human survival, truly grasps the fundamental problems facing contemporary humanity, and clarifies the new Marxist mission in the 21st century. Today, with the rapid development of capitalism, not only the relationship between exploitation and exploitation among the classes has not been resolved, but the differentiation between the rich and the poor between the classes has not been resolved. Natural bottom line and social bottom line. The dual possibility of human destruction caused by natural contingency and self-destruction caused by human practice coexist. For the first time, human beings face the possibility of total destruction for themselves for the first time. In such a situation, the pursuit of a better society for the free and comprehensive development of mankind must be based on the basic premise that human society can survive. This requires that while pursuing free development, maintaining human existence and building a beautiful home as the basic mission. The idea of constructing a community of shared future for mankind has truly grasped this fundamental theme of today's era, so it can become the fundamental idea leading the development of social history.

On many occasions, President Xi Jinping discussed humanity's military crisis, natural environment crisis and survival challenges it is facing. With these common challenges, we are required by the times to construct a community of shared future for mankind as our basic mission in practice. This proposal provided vivid characteristics of the times for Marxist theory so that it can play a leading role in modern social and historical development. We should, in a dialectical way, understand the internal relation between this proposal and Marx' liberation discourse, and deeply explore this proposal's expanding effect on Marxist theory and practical space. We cannot place this thought in opposition to the liberation theory of Marxism which aims to realize free and comprehensive development of humanity. The thought of constructing a community of shared future for mankind is Marxism's development under new historical conditions and has reflected the realistic care and historical responsibilities contained in Marxism. As President Xi Jinping pointed out in the Party's 19th NC report: "The CCP is a political party seeking happiness for the people and working for humanity's progress. The CCP bears the mission of making greater contribution to humanity." Constructing a community of shared future for mankind is CCP's dedication for humanity's progress, and Chinese Communists' innovative development of Marxism.

Marxism is not an abstract theory detached from the times. Faced with the common difficulties and problems of human society, constructing a community of shared future for mankind has become the strong call of the times, a basic concept of Chinese socialism aiming to facilitate modern human development in the 21st century, and a historical mission proposed in Marxism. Similarly, Marxism is not an abstract human theory detached from countries and nations. Without dependency on nations and countries as well as the cause of national development, the construction of a community of shared future for mankind is only a vacant and abstract theory. Therefore, another subject of socialism with Chinese characteristics is to construct a national community of Chinese nation while constructing a community of shared future for mankind, strengthen national unity, and realize the Chinese dream of national rejuvenation. "The initial heart and mission of Chinese Communists are to seek happiness for Chinese people and rejuvenation for Chinese nation. The initial heart and mission are the basic power motivating Chinese Communists to march forward." Therefore, we must "expand our education on national unity and advancement, enhance the awareness of national community, strengthen integration and interaction of different nations, and facilitate the unity of nations like pomegranate seeds holding together." The great rejuvenation of Chinese nation is the basic flag of Chinese Marxism in the 21st century.

The CCP is a political party armed with Marxism. Marxism is a strong thought weapon of the CCP. Accomplishing national democratic revolution and rescuing the nation is the realistic mission and initial heart of the CCP. In Mao Zedong's words, Chinese revolution and reality is our "target" and task, and Marxism is our "arrow" and powerful thought weapon. Since its birth, the CCP has been connected with the historical destiny of Chinese nation. In 1922, the Party's 2nd NC formulated the highest and lowest guidelines of the Party. The lowest guideline is the guideline used in the stage of democratic revolution, and its basic target was to eliminate civil strife, defeat warlords, achieve domestic peace, overthrow international imperialism, achieve full independence of Chinese nation, and set up a real democratic republic. Then we created further conditions to set up a democratic dictatorship of workers and peasants, remove the system of private properties, and gradually build a communist society. This is the first democratic revolution guideline thoroughly fighting against imperialism and feudalism in modern history of China, and set out the initial heart and mission of the CCP. The lowest guideline is the action guideline realizing great rejuvenation of Chinese nation. Under its guidance, China went through a magnificent period of revolution, construction and reform, and progressed from "standing up" and "getting rich" to "getting strong". Today, at the key historical stage when China walks from "getting rich" to "getting strong", the socialist thought with Chinese characteristics in Xi Jinping's times is gathering national will with the Chinese dream of national rejuvenation. It has sounded the horn of national rejuvenation, and as a new expression of the historical mission of Marxism's Sinicization, it has profound historical influence.

Here we want to clarify a mistaken view that the great rejuvenation of Chinese nation is an internal affair of China and has no bearing on Marxism. In the view of partial and dogmatic Marxists, the great rejuvenation of Chinese nation is a nationalist subject and is contradictory with the principles of Marxism, because Marxism advocates internationalism and emphasizes international cooperation and even the elimination of national boundaries. This is a fundamental misunderstanding of Marxism and has placed Marxism in opposition to national countries. Founders of Marxism never denied the standings of national countries in an abstract way or opposed to liberation of national countries. In the view of classic authors, only when national countries are liberated and the liberation of national countries is connected with humanity's advancement will human liberation and internationalism carry realistic significance. Engels clearly pointed out in the preface to the Italian edition of *The Communist Manifesto* that without the independence and unity of national countries, the international alliance of proletarian class and the cooperation of different nations for a joint purpose cannot take place. The national standing and humanity's general standing are not opposed to each other, and only narrow nationalism is contradictory with overall human standing. Similarly, only abstract internationalists adhere to a standing against national countries.

Among contemporary thought trends in agreement with the great rejuvenation of Chinese nation, there is a trend of combining narrow nationalism with cultural conservatism. People in such a trend are obsessed with traditional Chinese culture, and regard it as the culture criticizing and surpassing modern civilization. In this thought trend, the great rejuvenation of Chinese nation is a national revivalism instead of surpassing of modernity on its basis. In this sense, it rejects Marxism as a foreign theory, and denies Marxism's future direction of criticizing and surpassing modern capitalism. Indeed, there are some elements in traditional Chinese culture which can overcome the limitation of capitalism, but these elements cannot take effect internally. They require activation by external elements and a historical perspective of walking towards the future and surpassing modernity. In this regard, Marxism has insurmountable theoretical advantages. Combining the great rejuvenation of Chinese nation with Marxism which reflects on modern capitalism, and bearing the responsibility of human advancement in the form of national rejuvenation is an important result of Marxism's Sinicization. Marxism provided a strong spiritual weapon for our national rejuvenation, and our national rejuvenation provided the soil for innovative development of Marxism. We should resolutely criticize the viewpoint placing national rejuvenation in opposition to Marxism, and innovate and develop Marxism in the great practice of "getting strong". Only in this way can we increase the weight of our construction practice and provide world historical significance for the great rejuvenation of Chinese nation.

China's revolution once provided a successful example for countries in Asia, Africa and Latin America, and strongly supported their national independence movement. The great practice of opening and reform also provided a special living case of modernization for developing countries. China's path, theory, system and culture are producing greater and greater global significance. Our experience in the process of national rejuvenation is connected with socialism with Chinese characteristics and sinicized Marxism, and is contained in sinicized Marxist theory, Realizing the great rejuvenation of Chinese nation is the historical mission of sinicized Marxism. On the level of general methodology, it pointed out the nationalization process in the development of Marxism, emphasized the combination of Marxism and national missions, and provided rich experience for reference. Organically combining Marxism and the development of national countries will become a basic path of Marxism's development in the 21st century. This is a realistic pathway of Marxism and indicates innovation in realization model and development path of Marxism.

Constructing a community of shared future for mankind is the basic proposal of Marxism in the 21st century. Adhering to the socialist path with Chinese characteristics and realizing the Chinese dream of national rejuvenation is the basic mission of sinicized Marxism. A community of shared future for mankind and a community of Chinese nation have, in two different aspects of human society and national countries, respectively, proposed the mission of the times of Chinese Marxism in the 21st century. Relying upon the CCP's governing position and its increasing global influence, the above two proposals indicate that we are realizing the basic purpose of Marxism in a constructive way, and transform Marxist theory from the focus on war and revolution into a social construction and governance theory focusing on peace and development. They are an important development of Marxism under new historical conditions. They compensated for the insufficiency of socialist construction theory put forward by classic authors, laid the foundation for socialist construction theory of

Marxism, and formed a constructive type of Marxism. The formation and improvement of constructive Marxism will have wide influence on the development of Marxism in the 21st century.

As we know, Marxism is a theory unifying revolution and science. The founders of Marxism proposed to overthrow capitalist rule by means of violent revolution and achieve total liberation of humans. Therefore, there were two consistent viewpoints on opposing standings in the explanatory history of Marxism. Both viewpoints agree that Marxism is a radical revolutionary theory. One is an internal viewpoint of Marxism which praises and affirms Marxist revolution theory, proposes that only by means of revolution can we overthrow capitalism and realize communism, and believes that Marxism does not contain a theory of socialist construction or the possibility of walking towards future communism in a peaceful way. The other viewpoint also believes Marxism is a revolutionary theory, but it criticizes instead of adhering to Marxism's revolutionary nature. It believes Marxist revolutionary theory is outdated, and Marxism is a doctrinal revolutionary theory. For the objectors of

Marxism, revolution became the synonym of autocracy, violence, brutality, irrationality and blood. In the name of "humanity" and "civilization", they criticize revolution and defame Marxism as an anti-human theory. Is Marxism a doctrinal revolutionary theory? Can we develop a gradual peaceful construction theory within Marxism? How do we look at Marxist revolutionary theory, and the relationship between today's construction and revolutionary theory? These questions are fundamental in nature.

Firstly, classic authors of Marxism advocate revolution, but they are not violent revolutionists. Regarding Marxist theory as a violent revolutionary theory is either a misunderstanding or a distortion. If we read the works of classic authors carefully, we can easily find abundant affirmations of the peaceful path, and they never abstractly denied the possibility of a peaceful development path. The above point was made obvious in the *Preface to Karl Marx' French Class Struggle in 1848-1850*. There, Engels affirmed the significance of legitimate struggles based on the development of situation: "We are 'revolutionists' and 'disruptors', but we can make much more achievements by using legitimate means than illegitimate and overthrowing means." In Engels' view, Marx also did not consider peaceful and non-peaceful means as black and white. He said that Marx, through his lifetime research, made the conclusion that "Britain is the only country which can realize unavoidable social reform by peaceful and legitimate means." Here, peaceful means and social revolution are not opposed to each other. Lenin left a strong impression of advocating violent revolution, but in the article *Task of Revolution* issued not long before October Revolution, he was discussing the necessity and possibility of peaceful revolution. He said: "Our task is to help people seize the last chance of peaceful revolution, and the method is to explain our guidelines and their national nature, and tell people that they are absolutely consistent with most residents' interests and requirements." At the last moment, Lenin was still considering how to use peaceful means to "ensure the regime is transferred from one political party to another." It was only due to the situation that an uprising was put on the agenda. Obviously, the revolutionary and peaceful paths were not in conflict, and revolution is not necessarily violent.

Secondly, Marxist has not placed revolutionary theory and construction theory in opposite positions. Because of limitation of social and historical conditions, when Marxism was founded, proletarian political parties have not seized the regime and have not practiced socialist construction. So social construction and governance were not their focus of theoretical attention. They emphasized revolution and the creation of historical conditions for constructing socialism. Marx once said: "What we should do in a specific moment in future, and what we should do right away entirely depend on the historical environment in which we are living." In Marx' view, there is little meaning to discuss the recipe if we don't have a kitchen and ingredients. We cannot require classic authors to answer the social and historical questions they were not facing, and cannot consider Marxism as only a revolutionary theory standing in opposition to construction theory. Mao Zedong said that we should be good at both disrupting the old world and constructing a new one. Disrupting the old world is only a precondition and a means, but constructing a new world is our real purpose. Before the success of revolution, peaceful social construction has not become a realistic task. No theory is intend to carry out revolution for the purpose of revolution. In the beginning of the founding of new China, some people believed the CCP is a revolutionary party good at seizing power, but not good at governing the country. But history has given a convincing answer. Sinicized Marxism applies not only to the revolutionary period but to the peaceful construction period. It is the kind of Marxism which can realize revolutionary dream through effective social governance and push forward comprehensive development of society.

Finally, reform is also a type of revolution. To set things right and break through the dogmatic revolutionary theory, Deng Xiaoping proposed that reform is also a type of revolution, connected revolutionary theory with construction in a global perspective, and creatively transformed the Marxist revolutionary theory. Deng Xiaoping pointed out: "Reform is the 2nd revolution of China". Both reform and revolution are intended to liberate and develop productive force. "The purpose of reform is the same as revolution in the past, which is to remove obstacles of social productive force development, and rescue China from the state of poverty and backwardness. In this sense, reform can be called revolutionary change." After the founding of new China, especially the opening and reform, the CCP innovated Marxist theory based on the obvious fact that it is governing the country with the largest population in the world. Socialist theory with Chinese characteristics and the socialist thought with Chinese characteristics in Xi Jinping's times, as part of the former, are types of constructive Marxism in the period of peaceful development. We cannot place revolution and construction abstractly in opposition.

The theory of constructing a community of shared future for mankind and strengthening a community of shared future for the nation has fully reflected the constructive characteristics of Chinese Marxism in the 21st century. It requires us to view Marxism as well as the dialectical relation between revolution theory and construction theory from a development perspective. We cannot see the huge historical significance of revolution theory and construction theory if we neglect the relationship between them. Regarding Marxism as merely a revolution theory and deny constructive development from the revolutionary standing, or deny revolution theory based on the modern construction practice is not consistent with the dialectical standing of historical materialism. As President Xi Jinping pointed out, practice and theoretical innovation have no ends. The world changes at every moment, and so does China. We must keep up with the times in theory, learn about rules continuously, and keep pushing forward innovation in theory, practice, system, culture and other aspects. Socialist thought with Chinese characteristics in Xi Jinping's times has lifted Marxism to the historical stage of peaceful construction, and is the new form of Marxism in the 21st century.

In the speech on the 120th anniversary of the birth of former premier Zhou Enlai, President Xi Jinping said: "Revolutionary dream is our topmost priority. Ideal belief is Chinese Communists' political spirit. The CCP went through setbacks and misery, worked hard and finally made a success, because thousands of Chinese Communists were staunch in their ideal belief and revolutionary goal, which are still shining with bright light. We should learn from Mr. Zhou Enlai, never forget we are communists and revolutionists, and never lose our ideal belief at any time. The ideal belief determines our direction, standpoint, speech and action." President Xi Jinping emphasized multiple times that we are revolutionists and should keep our initial heart and inherit the revolutionary spirit. It can be said that the promotion of revolutionary subjective spirit in Marxism is the vivid characteristic of socialist thought with Chinese characteristics in Xi Jinping's times. Under new historical conditions, socialist thought with Chinese characteristics in Xi Jinping's times lifted the revolutionary subjective spirit of Marxism to new historical height, and transformed revolutionary subjectivity into strong spiritual power of socialist construction. It can be said that in a strong China, such a strong social responsibility and historical mission once again provided vitality for the subjective spirit of Marxism. The mission of changing history through constructive practice is the development of revolutionary spirit under new historical conditions.

Marxism is a theory used not only to explain the world, but to change the world. Marxism regards history as humanity's activity of pursuing their own goals, and a process in which humanity changes the subjective world while changing the objective in survival practice.

Historical materialism objects to the concept regarding history as a mechanical process of fatalism, emphasizes subjective thought, and regards historical research and process as a dialectical expansion process in which the subject and object interact with each other. As historical subject, humans are regarded as the purpose of self-fulfillment and the power of self-development. History is a process in which the subject takes part in, interferes with and changes reality. The history concept in historical materialism emphasizes the social responsibility and historical mission of changing reality, and is filled with a strong and practical subjective spirit. History is not a spontaneous process of cause and effect like the nature, but a dialectical process in which subjective initiative and objective restriction interact with each other. Based on the subjective historical view, we reveal the historical limitation of modern liberation through criticizing modern capitalist system. And Marxism regards as its basic purpose overthrowing capitalist production mode and realizing free and comprehensive development of humans. Marxism is a theory filled with subjective spirit of pushing forward social and historical development. The revolutionary subjective spirit is the most important spiritual heritage of Marxism. Revolutionary subjective spirit does not necessarily mean to carry out revolution, combat in the battlefield, and overthrow the current regime, but an initiative to positively change history and push forward social advancement. It is a strong sense of social responsibility and historical mission, a practical will of advancing with bravery and high spirit, and a responsibility of pursuing freedom and a happy life. Under the guidance of Marxist revolutionary theory and spirit, human history has changed drastically. Marxism itself has become an internal element of modern historical development. Especially, the revolutionary subjective spirit of Marxism was a strong force pushing forward historical development and social advancement.

Of course, history does not always advance smoothly, and there must be ups and downs. Faced with a series of disasters including the two world wars in the 20th century, a strong pessimistic thought appeared in the middle and late periods of the 20th century. It denied humanity's subjective spirit of changing history as well as revolution. In such an atmosphere, theoretical tasks were considered not as guidance of practice, but a game within thought, and a discourse and narration used to tell stories. Since the 1960-1970s, the subjective spirit of changing history suffered a heavy blow, the initiative of changing society was mocked by many, and cynicism and nihilism were prevailing. The subjective spirit of Marxism and socialism was widely criticized and questioned. By the end of the 1980s and the beginning of the 1990s, the collapse of Soviet Union and drastic change in Eastern Europe took place with profound historical influence. Marxism, which advocates surpassing capitalism and building a different path in future suffered serious setbacks, and the "end of history" became popular again. People holding the view of "end of history" believed that Marxism and socialism advocating surpassing of modern capitalism have failed completely, and modern capitalism and the system of freedom and democracy are the end of human history. They believed humanity cannot and does not need to change modern capitalism, and the revolutionary subjective spirit is only rational craziness of humans. Under the impact of historical events, Marxism and socialism went into a period of low tide. The revolutionary subjective awareness and spirit of humans to change history and reshape and expand themselves declined. The notion of changing reality and creating the future lost its attraction. Since people lost their expectation for the future, they also lost their passion and responsibility of creating the future. The mood of pessimism, cynicism, pragmatism and nihilism was widespread.

In the new century, especially since the breakout of the global financial crisis in 2008, world situation had new changes, and the thought trends of Marxism and socialism regained their popularity in the western world. On one hand, social contradictions and crises broke out at the same time in developed countries, and criticism against capitalism and the thought of changing reality attracted wide attention again. And there was a trend of combining theory with reality. On the other hand, the success of socialism with Chinese characteristics under the guidance of Marxism enabled people to see a diversified image of Marxism and the strong vitality of Marxist theory in social construction. With revolutionary subjective spirit, the CCP pushes forward the development of Chinese society and humanity. The Chinese dream of national rejuvenation and the thought of constructing a community of shared future for mankind have reflected a strong spirit of revolutionary subjectivity. "The Chinese nation is a great nation having endured trials and difficulties, Chinese people are a great group of people who are diligent, and constantly striving to become stronger, and the CCP is a great political party brave enough to fight for victory. The wheel of history is rolling forward, and the tide of times is moving forward with great strength. History will only benefit resolute fighters, and will not wait for those who are hesitant, lazy or timid. The Party must always work hard with a humble mood, seize opportunities of the times, and walk the path of long march in the new times." It can be said that socialist thought with Chinese characteristics in Xi Jinping's times has reflected the subjective spirit of Marxist revolution in a new historical stage, and is a vivid reflection of promoting revolutionary subjective spirit in peaceful times.

When modern humans are faced with various difficulties and society and history are developing rapidly, such a subjective spirit and willpower will play a huge role and involve Marxism in humanity's advancement in a non-revolutionary environment. The subjective spirit and responsibility awareness of creating history will become the vivid characteristic of Marxism in the 21st century. The passion and willpower, which were in a slumber over many years, were once again awakened under new historical conditions and in a different thought context, and will become humanity's hope for the future. As President Xi Jinping pointed out in Davos Forum: "Humanity's progress never has a flat and open pathway, and we are always advancing through difficulties. No difficulty, no matter how great it is, can stop our steps forward. In the face of difficulties, we should not complain about ourselves, criticize others, abandon self-confidence, or avoid responsibilities, but should come together to overcome the difficulties. History is created by brave people. Let's summon self-confidence, take actions, and walk toward the future hand-in-hand!" Socialist thought with Chinese characteristics in Xi Jinping's times is a vivid reflection of revolutionary subjective spirit. It will gather tremendous force and strong willpower to realize the great rejuvenation of Chinese nation, awaken people's sense of historical responsibility, form a common will to construct a community of shared future for mankind, and become strong spiritual power pushing forward humanity's advancement.

Reference

Marx, Engels. *Selected Works of Marx and Engels*: Vol 1. Beijing: People's Publishing House, 1995.

Marx, Engels. *Selected Works of Marx and Engels*: Vol 3. Beijing: People's Publishing House, 1995.

Marx, Engels. *Collected Works of Marx and Engels*: Vol 1. Beijing: People's Publishing House, 2009.

Marx, Engels. *Collected Works of Marx and Engels*: Vol 2. Beijing: People's Publishing House, 2009.

Marx, Engels. *Collected Works of Marx and Engels*: Vol 3. Beijing: People's Publishing House, 2009.

Marx, Engels. *Collected Works of Marx and Engels*: Vol 10. Beijing: People's Publishing House, 2009.

Marx, Engels. *Collected Works of Marx and Engels*: Vol 23. Beijing: People's Publishing House, 1972.

Marx, Engels. *Collected Works of Marx and Engels*: Vol 25. Beijing: People's Publishing House, 1972.

Marx, Engels. *Collected Works of Marx and Engels*: Vol 30. Beijing: People's Publishing House, 1995.

Marx, Engels. *Collected Works of Marx and Engels*: Vol 31. Beijing: People's Publishing House, 1998.

Marx, Engels. *Collected Works of Marx and Engels*: Vol 35. Beijing: People's Publishing House, 1971.

Marx, Engels. *Collected Works of Marx and Engels*: Vol 44. Beijing: People's Publishing House, 2001.

Marx, Engels. *Collected Works of Marx and Engels*: Vol 46. Beijing: People's Publishing House, 2003.

Lenin. *Selected Works of Lenin*: Vol 1. Beijing: People's Publishing House, 1995.

Lenin. *Selected Works of Lenin*: Vol 2. Beijing: People's Publishing House, 1995.

Lenin. *Selected Works of Lenin*: Vol 3. Beijing: People's Publishing House, 1995.

Lenin. *Selected Works of Lenin*: Vol 4. Beijing: People's Publishing House, 1995.

Lenin. *Special Collection of Lenin*. Beijing: People's Publishing House, 2009.

Lenin. *Collected Works of Lenin*: Vol 26. Beijing: People's Publishing House, 1990.

Lenin. *Collected Works of Lenin*: Vol 32. Beijing: People's Publishing House, 1958.

Lenin. *Collected Works of Lenin*: Vol 37. Beijing: People's Publishing House, 1986.

Lenin. *Collected Works of Lenin*: Vol 42. Beijing: People's Publishing House, 1987.

Mao Zedong. *Selected Works of Mao Zedong*: Vol 1. Beijing: People's Publishing House, 1991.

Mao Zedong. *Selected Works of Mao Zedong*: Vol 2. Beijing: People's Publishing House, 1991.

Mao Zedong. *Selected Works of Mao Zedong*: Vol 3. Beijing: People's Publishing House, 1991.

Mao Zedong. *Selected Works of Mao Zedong*: Vol 4. Beijing: People's Publishing House, 1991.

Mao Zedong. *Selected Works of Mao Zedong*: Vol 7. Beijing: People's Publishing House, 1999.

Deng Xiaoping. *Selected Works of Deng Xiaoping*: Vol 3. Beijing: People's Publishing House, 1993.

Deng Xiaoping. *Selected Works of Deng Xiaoping*: Vol 2. Beijing: People's Publishing House, 1994.

Deng Xiaoping. *Report on Revision of Party Constitution.* Beijing: People's Publishing House, 1956.

Collected Documents of the 19th National Congress of the Party. Beijing: Party Construction Books Press, 2017.

Xi Jinping. Speech on the 95th Anniversary of the Founding of Chinese Communist Party. Beijing: People's Publishing House, 2016.

Xi Jinping. *Xi Jinping On the Governance of China.* Beijing: Foreign Language Press, 2014.

Publicity Department of the CPC Central Committee. *Important Speeches of President Xi Jinping.* Beijing: Learning Press, People's Publishing House, 2014.

Publicity Department of the CPC Central Committee. *Important Speeches of President Xi Jinping.* Beijing: Learning Press, People's Publishing House, 2016.

Xi Jinping. Speech on the Forum of the 120th Anniversary of the Birth of Comrade Mao Zedong. Beijing: People's Publishing House, 2013.

Xi Jinping. Review and Conclusion of the Party's Construction Over 30 Years During Opening and Reform. Study Times, 2008.9.8.

Xi Jinping. Bear Mission of the Times and Facilitate Global Development -- A Keynote Speech on the Opening Ceremony of the Annual Meeting of World Economic Forum in 2017. People's Daily, 2017.1.18.

Hegel. *Philosophy of History.* Shanghai: Shanghai Century Publishing Group, 2006.

Selected Philosophical Works of Plekhanov: Vol 2. Beijing: Sanlian Bookstore, 1961.

Lukacs. *History and Class Consciousness.* Beijing: Commercial Press, 1999.

Sartre. *Critique of Dialectical Reason*: Vol 1. Hefei: Anhui Literature and Art Press, 1998.

Commons. *Institutional Economics*: Vol 1. Beijing: Commercial Press, 1962.

Terry Eagleton. *The Illusions of Postmodernism*. Beijing: Commercial Press, 2000.

Institute of Modern History CASS. *Selected Works of the May 4th Movement*. Beijing: Sanlian Bookstore, 1959.

Lu Xun. *Essays Written in a Garret in the Quasi-Concession*. Beijing: People's Literature Publishing House, 1973.

Xiao Qian. *Principles of Marxist Philosophy*: Vol 1. Beijing: China Renmin University Press, 1994.

Chen Xueming. *The Chinese Path*. Beijing: People's Publishing House, 2015.

Hao Lixin, Zang Fengyu. *Textbook of Historical Materialism for Party Members*. Beijing: People's Publishing House, 2014.

Luo Qian. *On Marx' Modernity Criticism and Its Contemporary Significance.* Shanghai: Shanghai People's Publishing House, 2007.

Luo Qian. Face and Surpass Physical Existence -- A Contemporary Explanation of Historical Materialism. Beijing: People's Publishing House, 2014.

Han Qingxiang. Nature of Modernity: Contradiction and Time-Space Analysis. China Social Sciences Press, 2016 (2).

Feng Ping, et al. Core Value Construction in the Framework of "Complex Modernity". China Social Sciences Press, 2013 (7).

Wang Xingfu. *Complex Modernity and Thought Liberation.* Academic Circle, 2015 (10).

Pei Zeqing. Construct Political Relationships with the Marxist Political Party as Strong Core of Leadership. Journal of Jinggang Mountains Cadre School, 2017 (1).

Zhang Xiaoming. Legitimacy of the CCP's Governance in People's Support Based on the General Trend. Guangxi Social Sciences Press, 2015 (12).

Marshall. *Citizenship and Social Class*//Guo Zhonghua, Liu Xunlian. *Citizenship and Social Class*. Nanjing: Jiangsu People's Publishing House, 2007.

Bai Gang, et al. Modernity "Beyond Modernity" -- Marx' Modernity Pursuits. Theory and Exploration, 2015 (5).

Zhang Ming. *Western Modernity Difficulties and Chinese Path's Theoretical Prospect*. Theoretical Research on Mao Zedong and Deng Xiaoping, 2016 (2).

Xi Ge. Marx' Capitalist Criticism and Modernity's Internal Surpassing. College Theory Front, 2012 (5).

Wu Li. *Review and Evaluation of China's Planned Economy*. Modern Chinese History Research, 2003 (4).

Postscript

To commemorate the 200th anniversary of Marx' birth, China Renmin University Press requested me to write the book *Karl Marx and Modern China*. Despite the heavy tasks of writing at hand, I pleasantly accept this offer, completed this book based on their requirements, and handed over my draft in time.

"Karl Marx and Modern China" is a grand subject which must be started from a good angle. The angle I found was: Why does China need more of Marxist guidance in the process of "getting strong"? In other words, I should explain the internal relationship between Marxism and China's progress to "get strong".

As history has proved, the combination of Marxism with China's practice changed Chinese history since the modern times. Such a combination enabled China to "stand up" and "get rich". Marxism's guiding role in Chinese revolution, construction and reform is an undeniable historical fact.

Now, China is standing on a new historical starting point of "getting strong", and is welcoming the great leap from "getting rich" to this new goal.

Then, does China still need Marxist guidance to "get strong"? In the journey of "getting strong", should Chinese people raise higher the flag of Marxism? Is the process from "standing up" and "getting rich" to "getting strong" a process when Marxism is weakened or strengthened in China? Which aspects of Marxism are the powerful thought weapon guiding us to "get strong"? These questions should be carefully answered by Chinese people in the modern times.

We believe the questions of whether we can use Marxism to properly understand the purpose and means of "getting strong", and whether we can realize this purpose through Marxism's Sinicization are directly related to whether China can realize the magnificent goal set out by the Party Central Committee centered on Mr. Xi Jinping.

This book intends to provide a research. Although we are aware that our research is preliminary or even shallow, our direction of research must be correct.

This book was jointly completed with two of my students -- Luo Qian and Jiang Guomin. After I set out the subject, Luo Qian prepared a detailed outline. Luo Qian wrote the preface to this book and Chapter I, II, IV, VII, IX and X, and Jiang Guomin wrote Chapter V and VIII. Chapter III and VI were written by myself. Here, I express my heartfelt gratitude for Luo Qian and Jiang Guomin!

It is our noble mission to write such a book with such a subject in honor of Marx around his 200th anniversary. As believers and researchers of Marxism, we are in great honor to bear this mission. We wrote this book with great respect, and with a sincere mind, we will humbly accept readers' suggestions and critical advice.

Chen Xueming

April 7, 2018

www.ingramcontent.com/pod-product-compliance
Lightning Source LLC
Chambersburg PA
CBHW081422090426
42740CB00017B/3156